CBGB WAS
MY HIGH SCHOOL

CBGB WAS MY HIGH SCHOOL

*A Rose Comes of Age
on the Razor's Edge*

G K Stritch

FCP

*Full Court Press
Englewood Cliffs, New Jersey*

Published in the United States of America
by Full Court Press, 601 Palisade Avenue
Englewood Cliffs, NJ 07632

ISBN 978-0-9833711-1-3

Library of Congress Control No. 2011923354

*Editing and Book Design by Barry Sheinkopf
for Bookshapers (www.bookshapers.com)*

Colophon by Liz Sedlack

TO THE MYSTICAL ROSE

TABLE OF CONTENTS

1

FAILED HIGH SCHOOL
AND THE PREDATOR

I WAS A BEAUTY—innocent, a rose without thorns—and waited for my life to blossom.

The first week of high school, the third day, I sat still in the homeroom in the cafeteria in all of my deeply flawed human nature, and looked at the poorly done and ugly murals on the wall, and wondered how to make them better. Maybe it would be best to start again with a clean blank slate. For the first time, I wore a new smock dress that my mother had made out of a pretty tiny floral print. I smelled the crisp newness of the cotton. On the crown of my head lay a thin band worn Juliet Capulet style, or so I thought. My thoughts were dreamily in other places, but from behind, a fellow freshman shoved me and said, "You mine." The hair band flew. I hadn't a clue what she meant. Startled, all ninety-six pounds of me stood up to my full five-foot-four inch height. "What? What did you say?" It happened so fast.

She repeated herself. She was about my size, with velvet cacao skin and could have been a fine-looking girl, but her face was twisted in hateful defiance and unexplained hostility that still remains a mystery. I barely knew this girl. Why had she say that? Why had she singled me out of all people? I was so quiet, so excruciatingly shy. I never bothered her or anyone else and don't remember ever having exchanged a word with this person except maybe a passing hello.

I pushed back. "Keep your hands off me." I never had a fight before and didn't like it. Heads turned, bodies shifted, chairs scraped on the hard floor, and I didn't want to be a player in that scene. Everyone looked. All eyes focused on me. Two young male teachers watched, not knowing what to do. The bearded science teacher with the hair down to his shoulders looked tense. The clean-cut one's shoulders moved back. I caught the eye of another black student, a sweet, bashful girl, who looked back with empathy and mournful, anxious eyes. If I had seen my own face, it would have worn the look of sheer disbelief, fear, and then anger. Enraged, I yelled at my attacker, "Don't touch me! Don't you dare touch me!" The moment froze; it seemed an eternity but was really just a flash. It was like the shock of a car accident, the slamming of the brakes, and the crunch of the metal, and the breaking glass. The girl was not expecting me to defend myself. I was too timid, too polite, so I surprised her, too. I could tell by the expression on her proud face. She pushed me, and I pushed back, and then it was done.

One of the teachers stepped in. That was about it. No

one was hurt, and the room was still, silent. Unable to suppress the tears any longer, my cheeks became moist as I ran up the cafeteria stairs out of that loathsome place and furiously stormed into the principal's office to vent, because I didn't know where to go or what to do. He was a slight, stern man, and his face was troubled and annoyed. His words cut. "You shouldn't have touched her." He provided no satisfaction to my dilemma, and I was suspended; so was the other girl. Someone handed me the hair band as I fled from the office. I dropped it in the trash and stumbled and ran the five blocks home to face, first my mother, and later my father. Naturally, they were upset but wouldn't allow pressing charges against her. "No one was hurt. Let's just forget about it," they reasoned. I didn't want reason; I wanted justice but got none. Instead, I secretly cried when no one looked. The girl's minister came forth and said she was a good girl who had never been in trouble, so the matter among those in authority was dropped.

Being that I was so sensitive, that event stayed with me through my four years of high school and beyond. From the moment of the fight, I hated Perth Amboy High School and wanted to go someplace else. My parents said no. They were both alumni, my uncles and aunts were too, and my two older sisters. Now it was my turn, but the times had changed. Race riots split the student body that first week of school, September 1971. I was probably the first casualty. I didn't know and didn't care to know what else happened. From that moment on, I felt lost. The school could have crumbled and vanished, and that would have suited me just fine. Quarantined at home on suspension, still seething, I didn't want to be at school and disdained everyone involved: the girl, the teachers, and those who'd stood by. I was embarrassed and ashamed and angry and afraid, inwardly bruised and hurt, and wishing to be invisible, but I had to go back. I wanted to quit and never see anyone from school again. I was shy and smart, the last girl in the world to ever have a fight. If only I hadn't been there! If only I had known what was in store for me that morning, I would have begged to stay home.

Academically, the school was less than mediocre at best. Given the chance of a good school, I would have thrived, because I loved learning. Ruefully, I was stuck, and that was most unfortunate. A private girls' school was in my mind, but out of the question, out of reach. Instead, for the next four years, my priority was to avoid the girl who pushed me. She wasn't in my classes, so there was just the occasional passing in the halls. Nothing more occurred in school, we never spoke or exchanged a glance, but that event was traumatic enough to considerably mar already difficult adolescence into far darker grays. I once saw her on the street with a cigarette dangling from her mouth and that same spiteful glint in hard eyes.

There were a few affable teachers, one being the man who broke up the fight. He taught biology, and I created gorgeously illustrated lab reports for his class, colored drawings of fish, frogs, and whatever other formaldehyde specimens we had been given to dissect. My lab partner performed the surgery; I did the paperwork. A squat, funny-looking Mr. Bloom, with a bushy, black moustache, was kind and engaging. (A few years before, he had married one of his students.) He took the English club to New York to see foreign films, which was fantastic. Manhattan on a weekday was a treat. I stood outside the movie theater and viewed the passing workday parade, absorbed the energy, and noted the dress of the passersby. This *was* the place. I liked another English teacher, an older woman who excelled in tennis. She had a sharp wit, but when I mentioned being an artist, a painter, she bitingly said, "Forget it—marry a rich man." A rich man? I didn't know men, rich or poor. Besides, I wanted to paint: rich oozing oils, soft sable brushes, rolls of fresh canvas, the good smell of turpentine, and linseed oil. I liked the feel of the brush in my hand, and the first stroke of paint on the new canvas, and mixing the paint, and the glorious rich colors.

Now, the one art teacher I had for four years was pathetically inept. She remained a gentle sort, but simply had no aptitude for teaching. She set up a still life, the same every year, and when Jill, my little sister, had her four years later, the class still used the same trite arrangement: a brown burlap background with various shaped bottles and autumn leaves, brown, gold, and yellow. For some reason, I was exempt from painting it. We could paint from pictures in magazines. Art classes, before this teacher, used to paint outdoors along the declining city's one saving grace, the beautiful Bay City waterfront. The views of the bay were unparalleled, but we were assigned the dreary still life or magazine photos. Other than that, there were no class projects, no assignments. I learned all that I could by reading everything, poring over art books at the library, and by visits to museums. A trip to the Brandywine River Museum stands out. Looking at the work of the Wyeth family, I marveled that such intricately beautiful work was possible from a person's hand, the glorious hand of a creator.

The helpless art teacher didn't draw, didn't paint, knew nothing about art history, and could not teach. She created no art. She was, however, politically well connected in the city. She shuffled around the classroom, sat her sad-sack self next to me, and sighed, "I'd go off the deep end if my husband ever left me." Her husband was a dedicated science teacher and resembled a mild-looking Vincent van Gogh. Surely, she had no cause to worry, but being inexperienced in wayward husbands at age thirteen or so, I said nothing and shifted uncomfortably in my chair. She slouched there and looked into space. She appeared slow, and her sorrowful face was malleable, like wet potter's clay.

My parents thought art school was ridiculous and made it clear they weren't going to finance it. Teaching, nursing, or secretarial work was acceptable to them, but not to me. I hated school, so how could I teach? Nursing required chemistry and blood, needles, broken bones, and hospital smells. Worst of all was the thought of sitting in a dry office all day surrounded by drab walls and monotonous music—impossible. I stubbornly refused to learn to type, my rationale being, *I'll show them.*

Talking to the guidance counselor was futile. She was as incompetent as the art teacher but insidious and slyly suggested that she would like a few of my paintings for her home. "How about it?" she asked. Absolutely, positively not! I imagined her house filled with hideous velvet furnishings. Let her get something to match. Quietly incensed, I left her office, not to return. She was another person to avoid in the school corridors. (Later, the guidance counselor would get into a fistfight with an algebra teacher.) My only hope, so I thought, was to apply to the tuition-free, highly competitive Cooper Union for the Advancement of Science and Art, located in New York's East Village. That would be the neat solution to my predicament, but getting into Harvard would have been easier. For months, I painstakingly arranged a portfolio of my finest work and completed the incomprehensible required projects and application. It was all I cared about. First thing in the morning until late at night, I was at it, trying to get things right. I had to get in. I had no other way and no other future.

I wasn't accepted. One project still confounds me. The instructions were to draw a hand holding an egg, which seemed aesthetically unpleasing. I would have liked something more poetic: a hand holding a flower, or a hand holding another hand, or a hand holding a book. With the Wyeths in mind, I drew a very straightforward, realistic, well-drawn hand holding an egg. I would have loved knowing what the selection committee was seeking and would have loved seeing their ideal. Apparently, it wasn't mine. If I had cracked the egg and let it slide down my hand, would the judges have approved? If I had done something decadent or slightly obscene or blatantly obscene, would they have seen the early work of a genius? Obviously, straightforward wasn't it, so perhaps there's the rub, and perhaps my Cooper betters were exactly right.

When the rejection letter came, my world went black. I had no support and nowhere to turn. As the English poet Frances Cornford wrote, I was "magnificently unprepared for the long littleness of life."

My parents were going through their own growing pains. In their eyes, my eldest sister Kris was staging a rebellion. She had left the all-women's, socially exclusive Finch College (now defunct) on Manhattan's Upper East Side to marry a musician; all my mother's dreams for the future had been in that one basket when it collapsed.

Kris was the most beautiful girl in her high school. Her yearbook photo shows an exquisite, Elizabeth Taylor-type beauty. Not only was she beautiful, but she was brilliant and talented. Whatever she put her mind to do, she did superbly. She was Mother's pride and joy, so it came as a devastating blow to the latter when Kris left college after her sophomore year to marry the musician none of us knew too well.

Mother's reaction was that of a tormented soul. There was loud, piercing wailing, the anguish of gnashing teeth. It was a frightening, deeply troubling time that cannot be exaggerated. My mother was miserable and in despair, and brought the whole household down with her. "How could she do this to us? We made sacrifices! She's throwing her life away." All this came with wet, bitter sobs and all the drama of an operatic tragedy. She was inconsolable; none of us knew how to calm her. We were young. The five children were in this order: Kris, Jaclyn, me, Keven, and Jill. Kris was nineteen, Jackie eighteen, I was thirteen, Keven twelve, and Jill was nine years old. It was the trauma of my mother's life and the first time I saw my father cry. Never was such a violent reaction seen before or since, not when my mother's brother was murdered, not during life-threatening family illnesses or after deaths. My mother's outrage was followed by a long, deep, dark, wrenching period of old-world sackcloth and mourning ashes.

My future was no one's priority. I went to school, came home, absentmindedly did my chores, and tried not to irritate my parents. I seemed to be forgotten. At school, I liked English, art, and history best. There was no need to study; nobody cared. I'm sure I was a forgettable student to most of my teachers. I painted what I wanted to paint, read what I wanted to read, and wanted to know the great Shakespeare. I read Kris's college literature books and the important plays—whether I understood them or not—and that was that. I couldn't see wasting time on what I didn't like. I wasn't going to do something practical that would lead to a job of quiet desperation. I was going to paint and put myself in the dangerous position of being a complete idealist.

I loved my family. I loved my mother, and I loved Kris. I

was heartbroken and fearful when Kris left under strained circumstances, but we'd always been great friends, and I tried
being loyal to her and a comfort to my mother at the same
time during the exile. Kris was my intellectual mentor. She
was an actress and read erudite books. She lived in the great
city, and she fit in with the best girls and best boys. She *knew*
things: where to buy a good leather bag, what to wear, and
what to say. I missed Kris and wondered where she had found
the strength to leave. I was sad and wondered if she was sad
without us, too.

At the same time, my so-called "best friend" turned out to
be no friend, but it took time to reach that conclusion. In a
toxic relationship, she would be a competitor, the sort who
takes your clothes, moves in on the boy you like, and finds
favor with the enemy—the girl who pushed me.

I spent the entire frustrating freshman year making an in-
tricate dress with a wide, circular skirt that buttoned from the
bodice to the knee. The sewing teacher, mean Mrs. Minchin,
had no patience for me, or my timid ways, and showed no
mercy. "You've done that wrong, *again*," she said, cruelly ripping open a seam and pushing the tiny blue flowers on white
cotton across the old wooden table. The material must have
been of good quality to withstand the constant ripping open
of seams. I hated the sound of the tear and her Général de
Gaulle nose and hard unsmiling face.

"Boys don't have to take sewing," I said.

"*You* can take that up with the principal," she replied,
ending my one act of assertion. I had been to the principal

once too many times, so I sat down, very much afraid of her. My ruthless friend the competitor bought the exact same Betsey Johnson pattern that had caused me such labor and tears and had her mother make the dress within a weekend, and she wore it the next day.

That freshman year, the WABC radio disc jockey Cousin Brucie came to our high school. I had no school spirit or enthusiasm for the event. He was booed, and I was beyond AM music. Culturally, I was six years ahead of my classmates, because I listened to Kris's music, the progressive music of the day. Maybe 1971 was just a bad time. After all, I was still reeling from the Beatles' break-up, another blow that felt like a betrayal. If they sang about love, how come they couldn't get along? The previous year, the movie *Woodstock* had been released. I'd looked forward to seeing it, but my mother had said no. It wasn't appropriate. Of course, my competitor saw it and had the album and all kinds of stories about what'd happened at the movie theater with her big pot-smoking cousins. She was allowed abundant liberties.

Senior year, enter the person who did pay attention to me and would be my first serious boyfriend. He was from a neighboring town and five years older. It began innocently enough, with a walk home through the park on a beautiful warm day. Mills rode a bike. He circled around me cautiously and slyly, like the lone wolf that he was. And I was the tender spring lamb. It was April, youthful April, the month that had brought this villainous creature into my young world like the drenching spring rains to come. He said I had a voice like a bell, and that compliment, and others like it, would ensnare me in his web of flattery.

Mills possessed no great looks, but he presented a fashionable image and a keen, calculating mind and worldly bearing, and he was interested—outwardly, aggressively interested. He was good with words. He knew how to draw out and flatter a shy young girl. "Tell me about your painting," he asked with his dark eyes and darker mind, and listened as if this was the most fascinating subject he ever heard. And I did. I told him all about my painting and my dreams, and he drew me in. He plucked his words cunningly and handed me a lethal bouquet filled with hidden nettles and snakes and scorpions.

My mother was shrewd. She didn't like that he was older, from out of town, and she didn't know his family. "Nip it in the bud," she said, but by then I had given myself to him, and was already in too deep, and didn't know what to do. I should have listened to my mother. Some months later, he insulted me with disparaging words. I was stunned. In the car, he turned and screamed, and I froze with a parted mouth and no words. Then he roughly pulled my hair. He was an angry young man, evil, a dangerous predator in sheep's clothing: soft flannel, washed denim, tweed jacket, and long curls. He came with a Volkswagen Beetle and a little beagle called Chips, Mr. Chips. I fell for his quiet voice and smooth laugh and the attention he lavished upon me that I mistook for love. The attention would escalate into a strangling choke. He beat and raped me.

After almost two years and not a moment soon enough,

I fled and got a court order to keep him away. I was lucky. Many girls, women, wives, don't get away. Restraining orders are not always a deterrent. Looking for love, I had gone into the world with a pure open heart and been battered. (Girls and boys, resist those who are jealous, possessive, controlling, explosive, and want to harm you. That person may kill you. Look at the newspaper headlines. It happens all the time. If someone hits you, let the first time be the last time. It will never get better.)

In that same devastating summer of 1975, my mother's brother had been murdered while he had been on a work assignment in South Jersey. Thieves had broken into his hotel room. He had fought back and been killed. My mother's family was a subtler version of the *famiglia* in Luchino Visconti's film *Rocco and His Brothers*—the excitable matriarch, the sacrificing saintly brother, and the eldest who befalls tragedy—the *fratelli*. My mother came to the clay tennis courts where I played to break the traumatic news. Shock and disbelief numbed me in the suffocating summer heat of that endless, brutal summer. The family was stunned into silence. There was little sharing of grief. Dark, drawn faces with dry lips and parched mouths were isolated in private islands of grief mixed with the unspoken shame of the newspaper headlines. At the wake, black- clad aunts and uncles kept leaving the room with the closed casket to step outside in the miserable August heat. Hushed, grim condolences fell unheard. There was no sense of peace, just a build-up of tension that filled the room to the breaking point, much as the scorching sun and humidity filled the oppressive air outside. Meanwhile, Mills lurked in the shadows, making himself inconspicuous, and temporarily slithered back under his rock. I was seventeen.

Years later, when I picked up my high school yearbook, I noticed that just about everyone who'd signed it had used the word "sweet" to describe me. I was so unhappy; I would have used the word "sad". Curiously, my friend, my best friend the competitor, never signed the yearbook. I was more popular than I realized, but I took that book and threw it away in an old, bent, beat New York City garbage can when I lived on East Fifth Street. I wanted no reminder of that dreadful time. I never went to a high school reunion and had few close girlfriends aside from my sisters. As for boyfriends, there was a long, long line, but it took more than twenty-five years before I entered a committed relationship.

Under my bed are six ten-by-fifteen-inch boxes of photographs, but maybe only three of the photos were taken during my high school years. One picture, dated 1973, shows me on a sofa sitting under a large oil painting, half the length of the couch, of a landscape of wildflowers with three figures seated in the grass in the style of the American Impressionist Mary Cassatt. I painted that large oil at age sixteen or seventeen and look desperately sad in the photo. Another photo is of a somewhat abstract watercolor cityscape that I did as a freshman, age thirteen. It is the only painting from that time that has survived. The painting has darkened with age and been damaged by glue, but it's quite good. Considering a thirteen-year-old did the painting, it's good indeed.

I liked one photo in my high school yearbook. I'm with the art club, holding a paintbrush, wearing overalls, and happily smiling, but that photo is only in my memory and physically in the place where New York City dumps its trash.

Ironically, Mills gave me my first 35-mm camera. I kept no photos of Mills, but when the Cobbe portrait of Shakespeare emerged years later, so emerged the image of Mills: the face and coloring, piercing eyes, and relentless stare all looked very much like him.

During our high-school years, my sisters and I, and friends, went to rock concerts held at varied locales throughout the metro area, including Carnegie Hall, the Academy of Music, the Beacon Theater, the Capitol Theater in Passaic, the Garden State Arts Center, Roosevelt Stadium in Jersey City, or wherever else a band might be playing. For the kids in Perth Amboy, one of the most accessible concert arenas was New York's Madison Square Garden. We could hop on the train and ride right into Penn Station, which connected with the Garden. When a big event occurred, kids from as far south as Bay Head would jump on the North Jersey Coast line headed for the city. We called the train *The Marijuana Express* because the smell of weed permeated it. The cars reeked smoke, and beer bottles rolled in the aisles. The train was packed with white suburban teenagers from the shore and points north, the last stop in New Jersey being Newark. Even if one refrained from toking, by the time the train reached the

Garden, the effects of the second-hand smoke were evident as scores of long-haired kids stumbled from the trains.

Yes, Eric Clapton, Steven Stills, Jefferson Airplane, The Allman Brothers, The Who, David Bowie, Fleetwood Mac, and Pink Floyd played. Bob Dylan ("In Jersey anything's legal, as long as you don't get caught") and The Band were most memorable with their unique carnival and circus sound. Lights dimmed in the big arena, and everyone settled down. The Band's musicality was like no other; The Rolling Thunder Revue broke loose. I usually went to concerts whether I liked who played or not, because it was fun to be with the other kids. Events were without incident: no fights, no weapons, and no metal detectors, just a secure police presence. In the dark, the kids lit up. The bands rocked, and we sat in a youth-filled world of guitars and lights and music and no cares.

In our senior year of high school, a whole group, including Mills and the competitor, cut out of school and went to Central Park to see Jefferson Starship. Lead singer Grace Slick had attended fancy Finch College, too. Even at Woodstock, in her white-fringed top and white bell-bottoms, Grace had the well-bred, intelligent demeanor of a Finch College socialite. She left before Kris (and Isabella Rossellini) arrived. It was a warm spring day in Central Park, and that was my senior-class trip. We reclined on the grass, happy to be with thousands of our peers having a free and easy American time.

High school, for the most part, had been a segregated place. It was nothing imposed; it just occurred naturally. At the time, about half the school's population was Puerto Rican.

The Puerto Rican kids stayed with Puerto Rican kids. The newly arrived spoke little English. There was a language barrier, and their world was a different world: different food, clothes, and music. The city had a small black population. We had not quite become multicultural yet. There were a few crossover kids, but not many. There was a black kid who claimed he played guitar with both Richie Havens and Jimi Hendrix. Kyle had a band with three other boys. The others all had long straight black hair. One of the boys, a tall Peruvian, appeared as an angelic apparition who transcended the inner reaches of that country, landed on city streets, and strapped on a guitar. The drummer was also tall and dark, with gorgeous Asian black locks all the way straight down his back. We said hi to each other. Those boys kept to themselves, and they all looked and dressed like rock stars. The too-handsome-to-talk-to Greek boy in that band had a brother who would later play with Guns N' Roses. Kyle was my friend, and I liked him and believed he played with Richie and Jimi, and that totally enraged the madman Mills to irrational, Othello-like jealousy.

Marvin Ramirez was a friend and a well-liked anomaly. He wasn't particularly bright, but he was nice and easygoing. He stood portly and oily, a downright ugly duckling with several gold front teeth. He possessed a relaxed smile, plenty of time, and he was an excellent listener with always a kind word. He seemed to be everyone's good friend: black, white, Puerto Rican, girls and boys, smart kids and not-so-smart kids, rich and poor, kids who liked sports, and teachers, too. He wasn't particularly interested in music, or anything else, though he was on the wrestling team. His father was a janitor, and Marv lived with his brothers and sisters in a wooden shack on the worst street in the city. He was amusing and cheerful, and he was mature. (After graduation, he became a well-paid city politico with no credentials other than his high school diploma and his good nature. His best friend was the mayor. The eighteen-year mayor and Marv and my former history teacher—who became a city council member—would eventually be indicted on federal corruption charges: soliciting fake contributions, conspiracy, official misconduct, and money laundering. The mayor would be convicted of misappropriating federal funds, and he and Marv would be convicted of mail fraud, election finance violations, and lying to authorities.)

Jesus de Jesus was an exception. He was a beautiful, olive-skinned boy with soft, glossy jet hair. He loved girls and was like a kitten skittering from saucer of milk to saucer of milk, gently licking up his fill. Jesus was not a love-them-and-leave-them sort. He took his time, and he was sweet and sensitive. I met him in the sixth grade. In his sixth-grade way, he romanced a girlfriend, and then, slowly, gently, without hurt feelings, he moved on to the next. Maybe the girls grew tired of his soft ways and warm kisses, because no one seemed to mind when he left. By freshman year, he was necking in the park with my friend the competitor. Again, that came to a finale, and he moved on to another friend. He stayed with that girl for a few years, and in the beginning of senior year, apparently, it was my turn, and his attention shifted to me. I was skeptical. I knew him too well and told him so. Nevertheless, young Romeo sent me, not one, but two dozen red roses. No. I insisted, and we stayed friends.

Jesus was intelligent and an enormously gifted painter. He spent the entire four years of high school working on a small canvas of Jesus in the Garden of Gethsemane. It was a well-crafted oil: anatomically correct, the hands folded realistically, perspective perfect, the drape of the garments accurate, absolutely incredible. It was complete and admired and envied by all. Then, Jesus de Jesus decided to improve on his perfection. He took a palette knife to the canvas and added thick layers of paint. The painting became something of a bas-relief, and that fine oil painting that had taken years to complete was ruined. After the paint dried, and it took a long time with all those thick layers, one on top of another, he put it on a rack in the storage area, and that's where it stayed for the duration of the year, and who knows how long after that.

I was a six-year-old schoolgirl when the president was assassinated on November 22, 1963. It seemed we had just returned from home to school after lunch when our stern, hair-in-a-bun, tight-lipped, old-fashioned teacher made the brief announcement. "Boys and girls, the President has been shot. You are to go home now." Something bad had happened, very bad. We were being dismissed unexpectedly early. How could this be? How could something devastating have happened to the all-powerful President of the United States of America? I walked home from school, Public School Number

One, built in 1871, with my older sisters and our friends. Along with the rest of the country, we watched the events unfold on black-and-white television. It was very unusual for our family to have television on during the day. I felt sad and afraid. My parents hadn't voted for Kennedy, so I felt bad privately. I wept silently as I turned my head from the television and left the room. I didn't want anyone to see my tears or know I was upset. I feared for the president's children and the First Lady. Where would they go now that they couldn't live in the White House with the big lawn and pony? I didn't like that the grumpy old basset hound LBJ was the new president and would be moving into the White House with his Lady Bird wife—and, of course, that was a highly eccentric name to a six-year-old—and his big daughters with the coiffed hair. I liked the little kids being there and shuddered when I later heard they would be moving to live in big, bad, New York City. It didn't seem safe or nice for a lone mother with a little girl and boy.

In elementary school, I had two best friends, one black and one white. The black girl was one of few black children in the school, though her mother was a beloved teacher there and her father would later be a popular school principal. Her father's family was from the island of Anguilla; her mother's family was from Maryland. Perhaps because the jovial Caribbean grandmother lived in town, we found Maryland the more exotic of the two locations and thought it charming and exciting to have a Southern grandmother. It was always pleasant to visit when the grandmothers were visiting and have some of Granny's attention or home cooking. Their home was full of love and music and company. Mr. Rogers was the director of the high-school musicals and sang at the Episcopal church. He was well known throughout the city. He was a busy man, but on Saturday mornings, he would take the three friends out for bowling, and that was followed by what for me was a rare treat: a McDonald's hamburger, French fries, and small Coke, icy and delicious.

By the end of grammar school, my special friend had gravitated toward the other black girls, and by high school, I saw her infrequently in the corridors. Our friendship never ended; it just slowly drifted away. My friend was a delightful girl with an engaging smile who grew into a warm, lovely woman like her mother and grandmothers.

Both my childhood friends were only children. The other girl was a kind, pale, plain child who smelled of milk and vitamins. Her light sandy hair was cut in short bangs, and her thick lips drew the cruel taunts of a ruthless boy who made the end of fifth grade unhappy for her and uncomfortable for me. We were relieved when he moved. She lived with her parents and maiden aunt in a large, wonderful historic house on the waterfront, once the rectory of St. Peter's Episcopal Church, the oldest Episcopal church in New Jersey, established in 1685. Antiques filled the rooms on the first floor: an old-fashioned parlor, formal dining room, bedrooms, and a long hallway with a floor-to-ceiling glass cabinet that housed dolls Auntie had collected from trips around the world. A screened-in porch with wooden rocking chairs occupied a back corner that had a view of the bay. The second floor had bedrooms, a kitchen, and a living room where we played school and library and watched cartoons. More bedrooms comprised the third floor, and the attic was stuffed with toys and clothes to play dress-up. The stone basement stored an old refrigerator filled with small glass bottles of Coca-Cola. I was very much at home in that house; we lived a few blocks away, separated only by the park that overlooked the city boat basin. We were together every day like compatible sisters, dear friends. Gradually, we gave up our dolls and backyard mud pies and skipping rope, and moved on to phonograph records and playing Auntie's piano. Seldom did we do anything daring. Once, we took crab traps to the old pier and caught a horseshoe crab, but quickly and fearfully released our catch. As we were walking up the hill back to the old house, an elderly neighbor stopped us. He looked at our nets, and then looked at us. "My, how pretty you are," he said to me. I was most disturbed by that compliment, as he had none for my friend.

By the beginning of high school, we, too, drifted apart. The competitor had entered with her worldlier and enticing ways that made my much less sophisticated, loyal girlhood friend seem bland and unaware. I allowed myself to be seduced away. The competitor had older sisters, and they showed her the ropes. She also had considerable spending money. Her aunt owned a phenomenal business, the largest of its kind on the East Coast, where cash flowed freely, and my friend the competitor worked there on weekends. She always had the best things and would come to school as a freshman wearing thick cashmere sweaters when everyone else was wearing plaid flannel shirts. Her closet contained racks of freshly ironed and scented white smock tops. Stacks of neatly folded jeans, including fashionable patched jeans, possessed the same scent of delicious fabric softener. Her mother spent much of her day at the washing machine and ironing board, patiently doing her chores, waiting for her daughter to come home from school. Shoes were stored in soft shoe bags that lined the closet doors. My friend had a museum-quality and extensive collection of turquoise jewelry acquired, also, from the aunt's business. Though she had so much more than me, she always managed to borrow something of mine until I had to ask for it back. I was the more petite of the two, she was a bit plump, and from time to time she would bring something back from her aunt's lucrative emporium that was too tight for her. My friend the competitor had a small mouth with crooked little teeth. A smooth round face contained round blue eyes. Her slightly rounded body gave the impression of a milk-and-corn-fed country girl. Long, straight, honey-colored hair was her crowning glory. I had other girlfriends, and occasionally, I'd still do things with my true friend, but we spent more and more time apart. Eventually, my loyal friend took up with a not-so-nice girl, because there really was no one else.

To earn money in high school, I babysat. At first, it was for the two little girls of an eye, nose, and throat specialist. The mother took riding lessons, and depending on the weather, we went with her to see the horses, or she went alone and I stayed home with the girls. That family moved and divorced. After they left, it seemed, I only sat for single mothers, usually a single mother with a little boy. There was one exception. Once, innocently, I babysat for a couple of drug dealers. Their apartment was cold and uncomfortable, the refrigerator was crammed with bags of pills, and they came home very late. There were stacks of weird magazines on the coffee table, porn. I touched nothing and sat there with my hands folded in my lap, scared to death, wishing I wasn't there. That job had come through a friend of a friend. The child was an infant that I didn't know how to handle, but she magically slept through the night. In the morning, I gave no indication to my parents that the job was amiss. I didn't go back, even though they gave me plenty of cash for my long night's journey into day.

My main job was for a little boy whose mother was a telephone operator for a doctors' exchange. Suzanne was well connected and part of an old family in the city. Her sister was married to a lawyer who came from a family of lawyers and judges. There is a street in the city named for the family. Suzanne's boyfriend was the son of the chief of police from a large township next to Perth Amboy. Lou was an ironworker, and in his spare time he rode with a known Staten Island motorcycle gang. Suzanne and Lou set up interesting housekeeping together. In the kitchen cabinets was stored, basically, an arsenal. That was an unknown word, but when I read the account in the *Daily News*, I learned what it meant. It was in the newspaper because Lou had been arrested for the murder of a man in an opposing motorcycle gang. Eventually, he went to jail. Suzanne never said a word about him, and neither did I. (Many years later, after his prison term, Lou sold incense on the street dressed in full Muslim garb.)

At graduation time, I won first prize in the city's Women's Club art contest. The winning painting was a realistic eleven-by-fourteen-inch oil of the head of a leopard with a black background. Jesus de Jesus had heard through the grapevine that I was going to win the class title of "Most Artistic." Finally, my day of triumph! Excited, I ran home and told my family. Now they would see! I suffered through the tedious graduation ceremony that took forever, very eager to hear the announcement, but it didn't happen. The boy who won was a friend and a good artist. He had just started painting in his senior year. I had been with the art department for four years. "Oh, no. What happened?" I muttered. I bit my lip and kept quiet. I don't know why I lost the title, but I do know I was humiliated. I sat in stunned silence as the boy's name was announced and felt like an utter fool. The four years had come full circle, beginning to end, and I was relieved when it was finally over, no more. It was done.

After high school, I didn't know what to do with myself. Without enough money to go to art school, I enrolled at the not- very-exalted county college and took all art classes: drawing, painting, sculpture, ceramics, weaving, and art history. My parents didn't understand what I was doing. I made my own art school. The teachers were smart, sophisticated, well educated, kind, and serious. I got straight A's and stayed for a second semester. The teachers liked me, and I liked them. I was videotaped creating a large abstract-expressionist Jackson Pollack-type canvas. I used a white sheet as a canvas and, with a stick, dribbled and flung black and then orange paint onto it. I wore painter's overalls, looked like an artist, and created art.

Lene Leder was an innovative teacher. She was an artist who lived in Hoboken at the very start of that city's gentrification. Ms. Leder said the sunsets on her commute home from Edison to Hoboken on the New Jersey Turnpike were superlative, the best she had ever seen, something about the chemicals in the air. I hung on her every word. She wore unusual art-type clothes and jewelry, treated me as an adult, and encouraged me. She had lived in Afghanistan for a time; her husband was a professor. She told wonderful tales of a rich life. The always-interesting Ms. Leder took our class to various painters' lofts in New York to see their work. It was amazing being in real artists' studios, their homes in the great city, the city of the art world. I wanted to live that life and do interesting work. Our last class ended with a marvelous feast in a Chinatown restaurant. Kris and Mills came with us. We sat at a large round table and dined. Lene pontificated and provided valuable advice: You can be the most talented person in the world, but you need to know how to sell that talent. I took her words to heart, but I wasn't quite there yet.

Lori Feld was another admirable teacher. She seemed

rather sad and silent, and resigned to the ways of the world, but she was kind, spoke softly with a German accent, and wore a few well-made dresses and sensible shoes. She was a weaver and had attended the Black Mountain College, but by then she was living in highly desirable Princeton, the golden treasure of New Jersey, not too far from the proletarian county college in terms of miles but unreachable in other ways. From her, I discovered the Princeton University Art Museum, located in that wondrous, ivy-covered, predominately Collegiate Gothic-style world, and learned to weave. A black wool wall-hanging with gem-colored inserts, woven on a large loom in her class, took me a long time to finish, and somewhere, somehow, along the bumpy road, it was lost.

At the time, the situation with Mills spiraled out of control, as he attempted to control and isolate me more and more. I lost valuable time with him and struggled to break away and save my life. Finally, after two years, I was free—badly shaken, but free from a monster. The last thing he did was to threaten me with a hunting weapon. The scariest thing about him was he fooled people, including my smart teachers. Mills was well spoken and polite, and appeared intelligent and calm, but he was stealthily, viciously cunning, and manipulative. One person he didn't fool was my father, who was a brilliant man and told me to keep away from Mills, but I didn't listen. I thought I could handle the situation the way I handled my problems: alone.

The mother of Mills was a mountainous woman: tall and broad, with an obscenely exaggerated bosom and long slender legs. She appeared like a wooly mammoth, so gigantic and bedeviled was her appearance. Her thinning, mousy hair was held back by bobby pins. She had few teeth but plenty of flapping gums. The sound of her harsh, guttural voice frightened me, but we spoke nary a word. A mother who spewed foul language was a complete shock: f'ing this, f'in' that, "pig, slut, whore, pussy," and then the "n" word. This vile character would have sent a sensible person bolting, but I was too agonizingly timid and polite and had never encountered anyone like her. She was a mass of uncouthness, a barbarism. Theirs was a bleak, broken household without joy, without light, with no food but what she stole from her job as a meat packer at a kosher butcher. There was no toilet paper in their bathroom. In its place was torn newspaper. I said nothing and kept my thoughts to myself. The shame of these events kept me silent for more than thirty years.

The small, rough father had not been with the family for years. There were two brothers: One was in the navy; the other was handsome. I wasn't sure who exactly lived in that house. They seemed to dwell in a scattered wasteland, an abyss of disharmony and rage and poverty, most notably a poverty of spirit. There was a pretty sister, she, too, with a lurid bosom, but she had escaped from the family and lived as a homesteading hippy in rural West Virginia with a group of rich Long Island hippies who owned property, houses, and horses there. She had a slinky brown dog named Pete. When she had a baby, she called him Pete, too.

The homesteading hippy moms thought beer was less

damaging to their kids than soda, so beer it was. They made a breakfast drink with beer and tomato juice. Naturally, they grew big stalks of their own pot. All was organic except the diapers. Bathing was done in a muddy pond, where Pete the dog or other dogs might join in, and showers were taken in hard rains. The log cabins where the homesteaders dwelled were comfortable, and some were built in modern architectural styles. Outhouses were used. There were no bathrooms.

We visited the sister; the hamlet was idyllic, with beautiful mountains and horses to ride and welcoming, musical people who played the mandolin and fiddle and acoustic guitars on porches at night, and grew green peppers and bright red tomatoes and crunchy cucumbers, and baked wheat bread served warm from the oven. That's where he assaulted me the first time, far, far from home on a deserted mountain path with no one in sight and no one to help me. This inflammable Iago dwelled in his own twisted mind; I was the bewildered Desdemona. It was numbingly unbelievable: striking fists, hard blows, black rage, vicious language, and false accusations meant to belittle. Choked, adrenaline and bitterness flooded my mouth, followed by heaves of drenching sobs. Stunned by terror, betrayal, and disgrace, I froze, frightened beyond endurance, and wanted to recall no more. After the attack, dazed, I slowly returned to the Volkswagen and sat with the brown paper bag on my lap that contained the just-picked produce and still-steaming bread, and looked straight out at the mournful country roads and hundreds of miles of driving ahead. I stayed calm and silently plotted a way out.

When the business of Mills was over, I went home; my family remained angry with me for a long time. Everyone appeared wounded. My mother was silent and stone-faced, and my sisters avoided looking directly at me. I was sorry for the whole bleak experience and angry at my own stupidity. Eventually, my mother thawed, as did the others, and Mills was never again mentioned. It was a painful chapter in my life, and I chose to close the book.

Before Mills, my mother had called me a rose without thorns. Now, I was a rose with petals ruthlessly, violently plucked, the stem exposed.

> *What's in a name? That which we call a rose*
> *By any other name would smell as sweet*
> *—Romeo and Juliet*

2

NEW BEGINNINGS, DOLLS, HEARTBREAKERS, EUROPE, TAKE ME TO CBGB

~

THE FOUR YEARS OF high school failed. Teachers were mostly apathetic, the guidance counselor provided no guidance, my best friend was no friend, and the art prize that could have justified art school was not to be mine. The fight in the cafeteria traumatized me, and then Mills abused and could have killed me. The school proved divided, segregated, split in half, so there were no dances and little social life, just sports, which I loathed, so CBGB—the famed rock 'n' roll club on the Bowery with all its clamor and activity and boys, boys, boys—was my high school, where nothing bad ever happened to me.

The most apt word to describe CBGB: crummy. It was a miserable, long, narrow space—pitch dark. The neighborhood was the pits, and down-and-outs hung from windows of the crazy Palace Hotel upstairs. What else could they do? Where could they go? That was their home. The racket came from downstairs and all the kids spilled out onto the street;

the Palacites had top-side seats with a bird's eye view.

CBGB, with its scarred graffiti walls, was a great place to meet boys who were interested in music and art and film and New York. Kids crammed the small space, and the air filled with the noise from the packed crowd and deafening music from the stage. Strange, amusing, theatrical, avant-garde bands called Suicide, the Contortions, and Richard Hell and the Voidoids played. Suicide featured a vocalist shrieking like one escaped from the harrowing gates of the netherworld, and a man on pulsating synthesizers and a drum machine. As the pair's name implies, they were on the dark side of art. Jill and I found the wild-haired, wild-eyed, and intense duo highly entertaining and funny, surely not the dangerous psychotic image one would have imagined.

The Contortions performed punk-jazz, but it sounded like a lot of junky noise, and a little, very little, like James Brown. The front man—he was really just a weird, skinny kid—sax player, and singer had us alternating between stitches and apprehension by his acrobatic, contorted jerks, growls, and snarls befitting the bahavior and noises of a tortured inmate from some wretched asylum. We stayed far away from the stage, because pasty boy Jimbo was known for nasty confrontations with the audience, and we didn't want to be slammed.

We actually liked Richard Hell's band. The songs weren't that good, but compared to the other bands, they were better. An older bald man with black-framed glasses and a black trench coat played guitar, but the other boys in the band were closer to our age and cute.

CBGB had a stage, a bar, and few places to sit. The safest drink was beer, because it came in its own bottle. Seldom was a trip to the bar necessary. Either I didn't drink, or drinks were bought for me. Probably I didn't drink, because I didn't like beer, and no one seemed to have much money. Surprisingly, for so rough a place, the bathroom was clean, maybe because so few patrons were girls. That contradicts every description ever written about the CB toilets, but it seemed clean to me. Of course it was so dark in there, who could tell? The boys at CBGB way outnumbered the girls, say ten to one, probably more; I was too busy to count. It wasn't a place most girls would like, because the atmosphere was so depleted and the ugly neighborhood was seedy and dirty and dangerous, a bad neighborhood, run down, old without charm. The drug culture had taken its toll: garbage-strewn lots, abandoned buildings—urban blight. The Bowery is synonymous with skid row, the skid row of all skid rows, but that's where the club was, right by homeless men's shelters, derelict bars, and boarded-up tenements. That's where the live music was, and that's where new bands played. And there we were, Jill and me, smack in the middle of it. We met all the boys we wanted to meet and always went home with a pocketful of phone numbers, dates, and new friends. Within a short period of time, we didn't have to pay to get into the club because we knew the bands and would be on guest lists. That didn't make us too popular with Hilly, the gruff club owner, the burly one-time New Jersey farm boy, but we only had to walk past him once on the way in, and once on the way out. We made friends—real friends—and friendships at CBGB that lasted for years. I can't say that about any other club. In other clubs, I had to watch my back and handbag, but CBGB almost seemed like a fraternity, a hole-in-the wall clubhouse in the concrete jungle, so we must have been there at an ideal time.

James was one of my first acquaintances. We stood next to each other and started to chat. He was a perfectly decent, attractive, and hip young man. For him, it was love at first sight. I liked mild James okay, but he was up against too much alluring competition. Too many other interesting, funny, cute, wild others jockeyed for my attention, and I had fun meeting everyone. (Poor James must have truly liked me, because years later, he would buy an engagement ring and pro-pose. It would have been foolish of James to marry such a half-baked bride—a girl who didn't know what to make of life and didn't know who she was yet, who had sense about only two things: drugs were bad, and one had to earn a living; other than that she was clueless about *everything*. Yes. James thought she was the prettiest girl in New York, he told her so, but that prettiness landed her in more trouble than it was worth.) In the meantime, with warm, melting eyes, James stood by and stepped aside, but he needed to wipe the stardust from those sweet, longing glances.

His father had been a failed stockbroker who committed suicide when James was still a young boy. The family lived in the tony suburb of Weston, Connecticut, where his stingy mother owned two houses on a wooded piece of property by the river and owned a home on the beach in Florida and acres of land in Vermont. James told me all that, maybe in an attempt to buy my affections. I found it ironic when his mother advised James to watch out for me, a gold digger. The gold wasn't James's; though he handed me a gold-digging shovel, I wasn't going to wait for Mother's demise. But old James was in love and willing to wait it out.

The mother certainly didn't help his cause. After taking two trains on an icy winter day to meet her, well dressed in a warm woolen skirt, sweater, and coat, I finally got to Weston from Perth Amboy cold, tired, and ravenous. Once inside her chilly house, she offered me dip and crackers as an appetizer, and then removed it from my reach saying, "I have to save it for later." Save it for later? For a rainy day? A bean dip? In my home, food was encouraged, so this was unexpected treatment for me, the guest of honor, and indicated treatment in the future. Ah, the blunt, unkind criticism of youth. Surely she had her reasons that I didn't understand. Nice to meet you, Mrs. So-and-So. Thank you for your gracious hospitality on this dark, cold day.

She said I looked like old-time movie star Linda Darnell. I didn't know who she was, so I asked my mother and hunted down a picture of the actress; I didn't look like her at all. I didn't tell the Dutch Mrs. Tight that she reminded me of Johannes Vermeer's astute mother-in-law, and that it made me very uneasy about James.

Romantic, puppy boy James made a similar food faux pas.

As I was walking through the park with him on a hot, sticky day, he stopped to buy an ice cream for himself but failed to ask me if I'd like one. Nice walking with you. Enjoy your ice cream. I took all this as a sign of things to come. Now, food is essential, and if one can't share food with a beloved, a relationship held out slim promise. Though I had little appetite back then, I knew I had to eat, and it would be meager pickings with James.

James played in a downtown band and lived with his band mates in an apartment on St. Mark's Place in the East Village on top of Trash & Vaudeville, a trendy, touristy boutique. Their apartment lacked part of the roof: The moon, the stars, and the sun shone visibly through the ceiling. I sat there in the snow, once, in the very *La Bohème* garret. The boys, all from Fairfield County, had a tent assembled in the living room that one used as a bedroom. A black-and-white photo of the group manages to make the fair-haired Fairfield Five, posed with guitars, if not exactly menacing, at least rocking. They took a great photograph, covered Buddy Holly tunes with enthusiasm and edge, and did some original material. Once, they opened for the band that would become our favorite, The Heartbreakers, or, once in a while, for The Senders.

A fast, slight, always-laughing, always-joking French fellow named Philippe fronted the fun, noisy band The Senders, who usually opened for The Heartbreakers. Philippe sported a continental look with straight, slick collar-length hair, and the band wore black trench coats and black jeans. He looked like a *noir* character from a French cinema classic, say, *Sun-*

days and Cybele (Les Dimanches de Ville D'Avray).

When Sid Vicious and his girlfriend Nancy were around, Philippe acted as their escort. Everyone assumed they all did the heroin thing together, so even though Flip was funny and sociable and nice and accessible to us, he seemed to be on the other side of a too-risky line. There was a big gentle golden retriever-type guy in The Senders with burnished gold hair, and I have little to say about Wild Bill except he was really sweet. He was surrounded by fast city alley cats, but even though he didn't quite look the part, he was comfortable in his skin and fit in anyway.

Meeting people, and being part of something musical and exciting that was happening in 1977, ignited my spirit and a world of possibilities. Long-haired hippy types wearing sloppy, ill-fitting, dirty denim and clumsy work boots were tiresome. Seeing girls and boys dressed in slim black and pointy leather shoes, girls with lipstick and all that hair of the previous years swept off young faces, and boys with sharp haircuts and clean-shaven faces was a welcomed change. Led Zeppelin and bands of that super-star ilk were out-of-touch money machines, dinosaurs. How could you dance to that music? Worse were the hippie bands: the hairy, boring, forever Grateful Dead.

All across the board, the 1970s exhibited a particularly ugly and awkward time for men and women's fashions. From high end designers, like Halston, Norma Kamali, Yves Saint-Laurent, and Vivienne Westwood, to the anarchistic British street youth—where Westwood got her inspiration—to main-stream, fashions were mostly unseemly. Hippies were old; disco had its moment under the strobe light: hot pants, stretch fabrics, flared pants and white pantsuits worn with open-neck black shirts and hideous gold chains, leisure suits in obnoxious hues, polyester, wide ties, men's three-piece suits, zippered jumpsuits, killer platform shoes, skirts ranging from super short to ankle length, kaftans, peasant clothing, prairie skirts, and earth shoes. Blow-dried, angled hair, or natural Afros, provided the mundane standard. Anti-fashion punk with its dyed Mohawks and facial piercing was appalling. On St. Mark's Place, where safety-pinned punk kids gathered, fear and revulsion led Jill and me to avoid eye contact or, better yet, cross the street. That look was never considered cool, ever. It successfully provoked disgust and intimidation. How could anyone want to look so revolting? A much easier look to maintain, a much hipper look, would be a simple buttoned shirt buttoned to the top and skinny black pants. Easy.

Immersed in dramatic black clothing that was perfect for urban backdrops and natural for me, with my dark eyes and dark hair, I took on the town. Black was a family custom; it wasn't a novelty. My mother wore black for evenings out, and my grandmother wore black, as was her old-world tradition.

CBGB was not pretty or inviting, but it was our Cavern Club. The Palace Hotel flophouse entombed the club. Maybe the Palace was something like the Metropolitan, where tender little Neal Cassady, that gone cowboy, holy punk, and cultural upheaval, lived with old Dean Moriarty. Reportedly, chicken wire separated the Palace rooms, not walls; that was second-hand information passed to us through our friend Brad, who, on a dare, had gone inside. I had no desire to seek entrance to that grim den. Such a morose place provided a home for the unwanted, marginalized, the down-on-their-luck. Men lounged in their cells and silently watched the live theater below, or they hung on the street and quietly drank. The kids took them in as part of the scenery. No Bowery man ever harassed me. When I eventually moved to the neighborhood, a naked Bowery resident stood on the sidewalk. From a distance, his attire remained undefined. There appeared to be a kind of sack around his groin. At closer range, it became clear, there was nothing at all but he himself. The man was out on a sweltering summer day clothed only in his skin and drinking from a brown paper bag. He didn't appear dangerous, just hot. I crossed the street.

Photos taken at this time show me as a serious girl with long, silky hair. I wanted to look tough and trashy, but I was too petite to look tough and too clean to look trashy. My direction was unclear. I worked at a temporary job at the public library and took Saturday morning classes at the School of Visual Arts. After the library job ended, I had to work as a waitress. I paid for the classes: drawing and conversational Italian. The moody, drop-dead handsome drawing teacher brusquely dismissed my work and remained unimpressed. Signor Rene Lavaggi, on the other hand, was wonderful. He was a sculptor and was kind and interesting. He put a little portable stove on the floor and cooked spaghetti for the class with his strong artist's hands, complete with wine, *buon appetito*. The conversational Italian was to prepare me for when, in the future, I traveled to Italy to see the magnificent art. I wanted to spend my youth being young, seeing things and going places, every place except the Palace, and meeting everyone. There were enough dark clouds in my young past. I was going to make up for those dreary high school years and push past the trauma of Mills.

It was my youngest sister's idea, and I happily followed her. Jill had gone to New York for the day with my parents, and they'd ended up walking in Central Park. She had spotted the New York Dolls' David Johansen with his blonde starlet-like girlfriend on a bench and came home and breathlessly told me. "Who's David Johansen?"

Jill showed me his photo in a rock magazine.

"Who are the New York Dolls?" I'd never seen anything like them, boys in a band who looked like young Rolling Stones, wearing dresses and makeup and big teased hair. They looked like boys, but wild, wild ones—kind of strange but still somehow appealing. I would escape into a new world, far away from the predatory, fake-hippie Mills and his lies and empty promises, a world he couldn't enter because he didn't know it existed. Mills was out of my life but always there in the back of my mind, ready to assault me again. He never, ever went away completely and remained my mind's stalker.

Before long, Jill and I were listening to the hugely influential but commercially unsuccessful New York Dolls, the energetic rock band that sparked a new generation of bands—and dancing to "Personality Crisis," "Trash," and "Subway Train." I took to the new and brash young music right away. The band was simply dynamite, firecrackers, and sparklers, a five-man razzle-dazzle with sweet Arthur hanging back. They were urban and raw and saucy. I liked it that the band had sprung from close-by and familiar New York City, not from faraway England. Mick Jagger and David Bowie were both interested and would go see the Dolls, but the band never made it. Aerosmith and Kiss and many, many others took an awful lot from the Dolls and certainly cashed in on it. The Dolls should have been *the* great American rock band. And they were, to the select few who knew them. Charisma, fun, personality, wit, excitement, and comic wild sexy smarts were rolled up in a great big fireball of rock 'n' roll live from the greatest city on earth—New Yawk. Wham. Bam. Thank you to a band that rocked things up at a dull time in pop music history.

By the time we began going to the clubs, The Dolls had imploded, but Johnny Thunders, its guitarist and singer, had formed The Heartbreakers, and we loved him and his band. "Let's go to New York and see these bands. New Jersey's such a bore. We'll get dressed up." That stellar idea, that excellent decision and stroke of genius, led the way. We started to go to CBGB and Max's.

The interiors of the clubs were so dark, you couldn't see where you were going. They smelled dark, like a leather jacket or stale T-shirt and cigarettes and alcohol. If the clubs had a taste, it would be what you got from a lick of a concrete floor or metal chair, or, at best, flat, bitter beer or cheap whisky from an empty bottle. There really was no atmosphere, not until someone interesting showed up.

The Heartbreakers played at Max's Kansas City, and compared to CBGB, Max's on Park Avenue South provided a bit of glamour, rock club history, and a vast improvement from the beat-up Bowery. At one time it had functioned as headquarters for Andy Warhol and the art crowd, so we were moving in the right direction. Downstairs was the dark restaurant with comfortable, worn booths and a great jukebox with lots of good time Motown. Upstairs were the bands. Perched at the door, collecting the entrance fee, sat the sharp-eyed club gargoyle, Linda Stein (the Ramones manager and, decades later, realtor to the stars). Hmmm, was it Linda Stein or was it Laura Dean? Short, portly, dark hair. . .Linda or Laura? Stein or Dean? Whoever it was, she liked us not. "We're on the guest list," I'd whisper shaking in my shoes.

She had no patience for the two of us who didn't pay. She was a tough Bronx ogre to get past, the troll under the bridge, the severe schoolmarm with the switch, the wicked witch to our Dorothy and Toto. After a while she just gave up on us, rolled her eyes, and grumbled, "Go!" Triumphantly, before she changed her mind, we hurried up the long, dark stairs.

The Heartbreakers always played late at night, early in the morning. We waited a long, long time, but they did finally show up. It was fun, really fun, to hear the band open the show with the great "Peter Gunn Theme Song." Excitement filled the place. All the girls and boys liked Johnny Thunders. He was sad, Sicilian, with a nest of wild, teased hair, a prominent beak nose, and mournful eyes. He had an appealing waif-like look and funereal, carefully executed clothes. A bandana wrapped his head and boot; that was new then, and everyone followed suit. His inspiration was the Rolling Stones' rhythm guitarist Keith Richards. The band played loudly and made a lot of high-pitched noise singing "Chinese Rocks," "Born to Lose," "One Track Mind," "Do You Love Me," and other rocking tunes. The music soared and safely transported the listener to a reckless, electric place—a place of big city danger and noise and young sexual energy and angst and fulfillment and stimuli and endless youthful promises of adventure and life, life on the razor's edge. The music made you feel like you were doing something bad, even if you were just quietly sitting in a chair. The music made you feel high, even if you didn't get high. The black stage was small and flimsy and weighed down by wires and cables and amps. The band emerged, played, pounced, and stumbled—Johnny in his tight jacket and impenetrable opiate cloud. When Thunders entered, the room parted. What was it about Johnny that made him stand out in a crowd or on stage? He had established himself as a star with the New York Dolls, had an image, a dark, brooding "too fast to live, too young to die" presence, and people admired bad-boy Thunders. The music was pure, reckless rock 'n' roll, and this was *the* band.

As for the drugs, no thank you. I was basically a good girl posing as something else—though the love of rock 'n 'roll was heartfelt and real—and I was happy just to be there with the other kids. Besides, no one seemed interested enough in me to share precious drugs. I don't know if I fooled anyone, but I certainly thought I looked the part. Johnny Thunders was a notorious heroin user. (Legendary survivor of rock 'n 'roll excesses Keith Richards still tours with the Rolling Stones; Thunders, however, was found dead in a New Orleans hotel room in 1991 at the surprisingly advanced age of thirty-nine. The cause of death was probably an overdose, but no autopsy was performed.) There are better ways to spend money than on drugs. If I had extra money, which I didn't, I bought clothes, lipstick, or chocolate. I was the Johnny Thunders of chocolate and would devour a box of chocolates or pint of chocolate ice cream, not satisfied until it was gone. Chocolate wasn't safe around me: smooth, silky, creamy delectable chocolate—chocolate, chocolate chip ice cream, chocolate milk shakes, neat bars of chocolate, milk chocolate, dark chocolate, chocolate with almonds, chocolate cakes with chocolate icing, chocolate mousse, chocolate that melted on the tongue, the rich, irresistible taste of heavenly chocolate. In my more innocent way, I understood the lure and intoxication.

My fear and loathing of drugs goes back to an exhibit the Perth Amboy Police Department once mounted in a downtown storefront. I was in fifth grade. On display were horrifyingly thick syringes, probably ancient things for equine or bovine use, and an extensive collection of weapons confiscated from criminals. I wanted no part of it. The following term, in grammar school, the police department showed our class a film featuring a young man who loses his mind after a bad drug trip. He's depicted in a run-down New York City tenement that looked not too unlike my first apartment. I didn't want to be in a place like that. I was scared and promised myself to never be duped by any charlatan who might lead me to such a destructive end. Injecting myself with a needle wasn't my idea of a good time. Nay. You had to be crazy to do that. Getting shots hurt, and if I lost my mind, my parents would be furious.

The summer of eighth grade, my friend the competitor produced a marijuana cigarette rolled up in tin foil. "Look," she said. She had older sisters and older boy cousins and a lot more freedom than me, so she was pretty advanced. She smoked cigarettes on occasion, too. I didn't know how to smoke.

"Wow," I answered, embarrassed to decline. I hoped not to get caught for something I didn't really want to do, and never once thought of simply saying no. After a few puffs, the smoke drifted out of my mouth. That was about the extent of my drug career. In a crowd with the joint going around, I did the same thing, pretended. I didn't like the smoke or the taste or the smell. The little papers were a nuisance, and a pipe was gross. The whole process was laborious, silly, and wasted on me. I disliked the dirty weed and didn't like the popping seeds.

A snapshot of Walter Lure shows him clad in a white jacket with giant blue polka dots and haystack-haired Howie Pyro in a pink jacket covering a Cramps T-shirt, upstairs in a backroom at Max's tuning their guitars. The Cramps did the best, mind-blowing, Neal Cassady-loving, sweating, groaning "(Get Your Kicks on) Route 66." Walter smiled and said hi; Howie remained elusive but wore fabulous clothes, copied from Johnny Thunders. Were they the first band or playing with Johnny? It would have been great having a picture of Johnny Thunders, but he hadn't shown up yet; and I would have been too timid to take it. I did have an original 8 x 10 black-and-white photo of Johnny and Sylvain, his former band mate. Both had been chubby then. The photo was an unflattering close-up, fleshy cheeks and crazy grins, so I threw it away.

A 1978 photo shows me, up against a New York University building near Washington Square Park, wearing a ripped T-shirt with a black leotard underneath and black jeans. My expression is purposely scornful. *L.A.M.F.* (a Heartbreakers's album title) is written across it. I made it myself. My lips are painted Chanel red. My face, neck, and hands are delicate as a china doll's (people said)—the original unpaid Kate Moss, all skin, bones, and angles.

Through our friend Brad, we met Johnny a few times. Once, at a friend of someone's luxury Eighth Street high-rise, in walked Johnny, his adorable little boy Vito, with big brown questioning child eyes, and his dishy but unhappy looking British (?) wife carrying their baby in her arms. I gently nudged Jill, and we sank into the soft sofa wide-eyed and mouths agape. We were in the midst of something extraordinary. It lasted a brief moment, but we were elated. "Can you believe it? What a day! What a cute little boy!" (Altogether, Johnny had three boys and a girl, and I wondered how his family fared.) Another time, we were with someone at someone else's empty Canal Street walk-up, and in strolled Johnny. He looked around, dragged his feet, and nodded. A drug deal was probably in progress, but, naively thrilled with the unexpected luck of seeing our favorite singer up close again, we just sat there on hard seats and looked at him. Then spoke the Thunder. He said hi, but showed absolutely no interest in us—and fortune truly smiled upon us that day, though we didn't know it at the time. Jill said that Johnny Thunders had asked her for a cigarette and that was the highlight of her life. I think she was only kidding. In that same room dwelled a thin, scruffy girl with dirty sandaled feet. I'd see her around.

I had a "date" at Max's with Tony Machine, the drummer for The Heartbreakers, for a while. He was more normal than wild looking, donned in black with straight brown hair and a large nose. He drank. We sat in a booth, and he became drunker and drunker, and could have been anyplace with anyone and he wouldn't have known it. I tried to talk to him. He did manage to say he was a doorman at a Gramercy Park building and had a small apartment there, not far from Max's. Gramercy Park is a marvelous, historic Old New York enclave, so to live there was the epitome of luck. I wanted to live there, too. Maybe he could tell me how. Only residents of the area's select townhouses possess keys to a beautiful fenced and gated private park—the oldest private park in the United States, and the only one left in New York City. Throughout his drunkenness, he slurred over and over that he'd come to New Jersey to take me to a drive-in movie. "Yeah. I'll take you to the drive-in over in Jersey," he mumbled. "The salt marshes of Jersey." Down he slid, and I left. The second date never happened. It didn't matter. If one date didn't work out, there were others waiting.

Mr. Syl Sylvain and I got together several times, and that included a trip to Playland in Times Square. It was a honky-tonk amusement arcade with photo booths and games, such as the metal arm in a glass box that picks up and drops trinkets. I didn't like being there much and felt slightly insulted to be out on such a rinky-dink date, but we took black-and-white photos in the booth, laughed at the four poses, and got on well. I thought he liked me, and my normally shy self opened up to his boisterous mien. We walked through Central Park at dusk, just when scores of rats scuttle about, and strolled past Bloomingdale's, so we'd walked all across town, and I felt like a real New Yorker. Short, dark Syl had a mop of dark, tight curls and an exuberant personality. He appeared very worldly, very conversational. The former New York Doll had a large wooden dollhouse in his Chelsea apartment on Eighth Avenue. Things went along just fine. I felt

I'd found a friend, and we talked a lot, but the last date ended abruptly. We'd stopped at a steamy West Village coffee shop where the waitress spoke French. I ate nothing; I was still too shy. Perhaps I just watched him eat. The details remain unclear but apparently, he had better things to do with his time—like go on to another date—and told me to go home. He hurt my feelings, and I didn't like him after that, but things brightened quickly.

The same evening of the failed date, two delightful young homosexual boys escorted me to the Crisco Disco. I don't remember where or how we met, but they looked safe and polite. I was wearing a new dress, and they'd asked if I wanted to go. Sure. That would be fun. I had no place else to go except home, and my parents were away, so I could stay out all night. A big painting of a slice of cherry pie adorned the wall, and the DJ booth was an oversized Crisco can. The Crisco was a blast, and we danced until dawn. I stood out as the belle of the ball in a red knit dress from Trash. I was the only belle; the others were all boys. Tired but happy, the boys took me out for breakfast, and then I got on the bus and went home.

A black-and-white photo dated December 24, 1978, shows a black leather-jean-clad Sylvain on one end of a bed, a black leather-jean-clad me on the other, Jill, and photographer Gary Green sandwiched in between. Gary took the photo in his small Fifth Avenue apartment. Syl and Gary were very good friends. Syl had given Gary the apartment; it had once been his. Behind us on the wall is a well-known photo of rocking rockabilly Robert Gordon that Gary had taken and that was used as an album cover. The small, intense, very dark-eyed, slick-haired Gary liked Jill, but it was one-sided. Jill and Gary look skeptical, Syl looks young and happy, and I have a big smile. The picture was taken months before the sour date. Gary had given us each a glass of Courvoisier that cold Christmas Eve. Wanting to emulate our suave host, we drank it as if brandy was our drink of choice. Apparently, they liked it. We did not. It burned, a strong and thick, grandfatherly, foreign drink. We called it old man's juice, and that was the first and last time for cognac.

Sylvain dispensed some valuable information. "Never tip a cabbie more than a quarter. They all own their own cabs." Wow. I thought to myself. Here I was giving away hard-earned dollars to rich cab drivers. Being that Syl was a seasoned New Yorker, I thought he knew what he was talking about and put his lesson to the test. As Jill and I were leaving a taxi at Penn Station, I gave the driver a quarter. To say he hit the roof was putting it mildly. The cabbie's face turned purple with rage, and he swore loud enough to wake up the whole block, but being that it was so late, there was no one to hear him, and the two of us scurried away as fast as our high heels would carry us, lesson learned.

What became of the black-and-white photos from the Playland photo booth? They probably went the way of so many other photos, tossed away, but I did keep them for a long time.

In the summer of 1978, our parents took Jill and me on a European vacation. We spent a week at a resort on the island of Palma de Mallorca. Photos show bougainvillea-covered villas on sprawling estates, and shuttered windows on peach-colored buildings. We headed to the shops, stopped at the many fashionable boutiques, and ogled the footwear. The Euros were oh-so-chic—not a sneaker or baggy jean in sight. Our first day there, our first morning, I spent all my money on two pairs of black Spanish boots. One pair was snakeskin, with a three-inch heel. The other pair was knee-high leather, with heels so high I could never wear them, though I tried. Almost as quickly, Jill spent all her money on shoes, too. One pair had a four-inch heel. They were red, strappy high-heeled sandals that barely contained the foot. They were also quite impossible to wear. After that shopping spree, we were broke and about ready to go home. Instead, we spent days on the hot sand, giggling at Euro beach etiquette, and nights in the packed clubs, watching Spaniards, Brits, and Germans smoke and drink, and smoke and drink some more. We were the only Americans there. I won a bottle of Spanish sparkling wine at a dance contest and must have put on a spectacular show to pull that off: shimmy, shimmy, shake, shake, shake in my snakeskin pants and new boots. Three tanned soccer-playing Brits were staying at our hotel; we named them Irk, Dirk, and Jerk. Judging by their names, we weren't too impressed, but they spoke English. They were well-muscled athletes, not really our type. We acted as if we were in Europe without parents, two sophisticates seeing the world on their own. Our parents had left us to our own amusements.

The second week of our vacation, we cruised from Spain to the ancient Mediterranean port cities of Tunis, Valetta, Messina, Naples, Ligurian Genoa, and Côte-d'Azur Toulon. Almost all the other passengers were older Europeans, with the exception of a large group of loud young people from California with whom we had nothing in common. Announcements on the ship were made in several languages, and they came frequently during the day and at night. *Bonne nuit.* *Buenas noches. Buona sera.* Good evening. Our only on-board friend was a young Swiss fellow who spoke little English but liked the same music that we did and sported an expensive hip look. He smoked cigarettes and drank. We sat with him in the evening, he smoked away one cigarette after another, and I won another bottle of that same Spanish sparkling wine at the ship's disco doing my downtown New York–Perth Amboy–Motown girl shimmy. The Swiss boy's parents were nowhere in sight either. We took photos of the European boys because we liked their nicely tailored, groovy clothes.

Tunis is a Muslim city. The day was hot and dry in the clean, bleached capitol of Tunisia. It was a thrill being on the exotic African continent, looking out at the sea. The ship's passengers were advised to dress modestly.

Jill wore white shorts and red high heels. My white sleeveless dress blew in the desert wind. The few Tunisian women on the streets were covered in veils, in white, from their heads to their sandals. A photo remains of children and their donkey. The kids stopped to look at us.

In Malta—place of the shipwreck of the Apostle Paul—we made pals with a young, dark-haired Russian who worked on the ship. We sat together in a near-empty outdoor café, where he smoked cigarette after cigarette and drank foul black coffee. By the end of the afternoon, we tired of trying to communicate with him and of the cigarettes and his cigarette smoke. He didn't have much English, and we had no Russian.

Following a Caravaggio path from Malta to Sicily, Lampedusa's land of the scorching sun and island of mystery, there was slightly more activity in Messina, and we met a group of boys on the parched street and took their picture. A mustached fellow wore a military uniform, one curly-haired blonde Adonis a loincloth. In another photo, you can see they are the shortest shorts, more like underpants or a diaper, ever worn by a male. We moved on to the fish market and took photos of the giant swordfish.

The cruise ship transported us to the other Kingdom of the Two Sicilies, Naples. Ancient *Neápolis*, the romantic *Napoli* of songs and beautiful harbor scenes, Naples, known for its depredations and poverty—and yet another place on the Caravaggio map—was sadly seedy. Narrow alleys housed cheap shops with cheap wares, and discarded cigarettes and cigarette packs littered the streets. We wandered the great crooked "sinful" streets that Victorian Arthur Hugh Clough mentioned long ago and felt safe once we returned to the ship. Later, our parents escorted us on the ferry going to the Isle of Capri. The shoes of a saucy, cigarette-smoking Neapolitan caught our attention, and that picture of our little *L'Avventura* remains in my box of photographs, next to one of Vesuvius rising through the sea haze.

Up the coast, in the beautiful and wealthy northern city of Genoa, everything was closed, and the streets were clean. A plaque displayed the name *Cristoforo Columbo.* Sitting in front of a gushing fountain, my pretty, curly-haired mother smiles.

Photos of Toulon show an outdoor market and fishing port. Jill and I ambled and ate delicious cold French pizza with black olives at an outdoor Saturday market. A nattily dressed old woman walked across the photo of Jill, dressed in jeans and a pink silk nightshirt, standing by the boats. In most of these photos, Jill looks down at her feet or unhappily away from the camera. Sometimes, she grew annoyed with my picture taking but was always eager to see the developed photos. I look sulky. My parents enjoyed the trip, and it remained a favorite for them. The sea was as smooth as glass, they remarked contentedly, and the ancient black sky twinkled with stars. I felt guilty because I hadn't loved the trip as they had. Jill and I were bored silly and more interested in what was going on downtown.

We didn't visit any of the great bastions of Renaissance art; most of the cities we visited were deserted, and everything seemed tightly shuttered. It was vacation time for the Europeans. They were away at the beaches or in the country, probably smoking their heads off, drinking foul coffee, and finishing it all off with more cigarettes, more drinks, more coffee. I gathered what little I could of European life but didn't have many occasions to use Signor Lavaggi's conversational lessons.

On our last night of the endless cruise, our grizzled waiter, who had been lurking around the entire trip, grinning an unpleasant grin, secretly ducked under the table and put Jill's foot in his mouth. Jill bolted upright. Horrified, she let out a scream, we looked at each other, and then we burst out laughing and named the waiter Footius. Tired of trying to understand all the accents, weary of the dour, chain-smoking, foot-snatching, black coffee-drinking Europeans, homesick for familiar places, we were ready to get back to wholesome New York, downtown, the center of our universe.

> *Crabbed age and youth cannot live together:*
> *Youth is full of pleasure, age is full of care;*
> *Youth like summer morn, age like winter weather;*
> *Youth like summer brave, age like winter bare.*
> *Youth is full of sport, age's breath is short;*
> *Youth is nimble, age is lame;*
> *Youth is hot and bold, age is weak and cold;*
> *Youth is wild, and age is tame.*

> —*The Passionate Pilgrim, XII*

3

PUBLIC TRANSPORT, ANDY WARHOL,
BLONDIE, PATTI, AND LENNY

❧

THE "BRIDGE AND TUNNEL" CROWD refers to those who come from outside the city, by bridge and tunnel, to go to Manhattan. It derogatorily implies that you're not one of the inner circle, that you don't have the finances, the intellect, or the wit to live in Manhattan. If I had known that term, I would have bristled, because I definitely desired the inner sphere. Back in 1977, Jill and I went back and forth to New York from Perth Amboy, dressed up, and always with high heels, via bridge, tunnel, turnpike, ferry, wooden rowboat, any way we could; like *George Washington Crossing the Delaware*, we were determined to get across. Our feet were lightly covered in European leather, and our young, romantic hearts were encased in Manhattan bedrock. We were never really casually dressed, sneaker-shod girls. An early favorite outfit was a pink satin antique slip that I wore as a dress—and it looked like a dress—with antique red satin, T-strapped heels. It was a doll's outfit, soft and feminine. There I was, running around New York in someone's old slip. A little later, I would wear black leather pants, ridiculously enough, on hot summer days. Image mattered and provided a key to entry. We spent much time and trouble finding the right clothes. The sought-after garments hardly appeared on department store racks. We searched thrift stores for specific items—leopard print, zebra stripes, and black leather—and then altered the clothes to fit. Trendy city boutiques were usually far too expensive and few (unlike today, when every kid in suburbia has access to piles of black, stretchy, formfitting apparel and fierce stilettos, courtesy of the local mall).

Jill was an expert makeup artist, and she applied our makeup. I'd previously thought wearing makeup was something like cheating, but I gladly turned over my willing face. I should have watched how she did it, but I contentedly placed myself in her capable hands and didn't look until she showed me the finished results in the mirror. She knew how to contour the face and accentuate the eyes and lips. She was like a silky sponge that absorbed fashion trends almost before they hit the magazines. We attracted attention, coming and going wherever we went. Sometimes we took the train, on weekends our father drove into the city during the day, but most often we relied on the bus, because the first New Jersey Transit stop was on our corner. Often, the driver wouldn't charge us the fares. We were the first passengers, two pretty, petite girls dressed to suit our own private world. The bus drivers liked us. We lit up their route and were a far cry from the run-of-the-mill tired commuter. I imagine we provided a little fantasy, and the drivers went out of their way to accommodate two such amusing cream puffs. Once, my string of pearls broke. The bus driver pulled over. The passengers looked around, alarmed. "Can I go to the store across the street to get something to fix it, miss?" he asked pleadingly.

Mister, are you nuts? These passengers are going to have a fit. You have a bus to drive to New York. I said, "No, thanks, but it's okay," and picked up the few pearls before they rolled down the aisle, hoping to avoid a mutiny, and blushed as I turned my head toward the window.

Strangers were curious and enthusiastic about us. In the city, we waited for a cab, and a limo stopped and drove us to our destination. Why? Maybe he thought we'd be famous; I don't know. Maybe it was our youth. Maybe we did what others wanted to do. Heads turned. At times, we were treated like up-and-coming stars and had many positive experiences. Sometimes, our avant-garde attire was misunderstood and attracted unwanted catcalls, but never anything more than that. People seemed to be rooting for us, the Frou-Frous. They weren't sure what the game was, but they seemed to be on our side. When we revealed ourselves to be soft-spoken ladies, we mystified our adoring public all the more.

Before the move to East Fifth Street between Second and Third Avenues in the East Village, we were in the humble position of relying on mass transportation for our evenings at the clubs, not so easy and oh so pedestrian. Like Cinderella, we had to leave at the chime of midnight; sometimes we had to leave before the band came on. The last bus back to Perth Amboy was at 12:30 a.m. The train left later, at 3:00, but we had to take a cab home from Metro Park, a few towns over, and that was costly and risky because there might be no cabs. One night, to our great dismay, we missed the train and had to get home to our parents. Jill started to cry. "Don't worry, Jill," said big sister. "We'll take a cab." A kindly New York City cabbie agreed to drive us the thirty miles to New Jersey. I didn't have enough cash, the fare was fifty or sixty dollars, but the elderly driver said he'd take a check. He waited while I ran inside without waking up our parents to get my check-book to pay him. The big-hearted driver certainly could have refused the sixty-mile 3:00 a.m. round trip, and the two little socialites would have been in big trouble.

To enter New York City through the Port Authority Bus Terminal on Forty-second Street was to enter a place between purgatory and hell. At that time, the Port Authority was an unofficial shelter for the homeless and mentally ill. Vagrants loitered in the building and asked for money. Men and women were bundled in layers of filthy rags and clothing, asleep, trying to keep warm on the hard, cold floors. We tip-toed in our dainty shoes past the odoriferous human bodies, trying to ignore the comments and pleas, and felt safe only when we were outside the building, on the street, waiting for a taxi, and experienced a combination of pity and fear and disgust and guilt and relief.

Of course, life in dismal New Jersey mortified us, and we thrilled when we made New York friends. Not everyone we met at CBGB became famous or infamous. Regulars Brad and Bobby Beat became fast friends. They were good Jewish boys who loved rock 'n' roll. Brad drummed for a band named The Blessed and deemed us "goddesses." Smart, sharp, cute, immaculate Brad was smitten by Jill and was a valuable friend who provided lots of introductions to people as diverse as photographer Francesco Scavullo, known for his *Cosmopolitan* magazine covers and celebrity portraits, and a young long-haired Mr. Mellon (as in the financial firm), who sported an opened Hawaiian print shirt. Jill and I were unimpressed. Upstairs in a backroom at Max's, when the swarthy Scavullo slid into the seat next to Jill, she got up and moved away. "Watermelon needs a new shirt," she whispered. "He's always wearing the same one."

Brad was a genuinely all-around nice guy. He looked like a doll, with curly hair and tight black jeans and pointy shoes. He was so young and so spanking clean that even Linda Lorna Doonestein liked him, but she liked all the boys. She was Miss Gulch to us but sweet as honey to Brad. She smiled at him, and we stood close to his heels when we ran up those stairs.

Bobby worked at CBGB and was one of our first friends, a diminutive, curly-haired boy, thoughtful, sad, and young. He had a big crush on Jill, too. She tolerated him for a while, but as we began to know more people, we gradually left him behind. He worshipped Johnny Thunders and worked as his roadie. (Eventually, much later, he went the H route and died, that sweet sad little boy with the baby face and frail body.)

Randolph Freds was probably the first person we spoke

to at CBGB; Jill talked to him initially. He was a master heavy-metal musician. His best friend and fellow band member Zeus, who looked like a Robert Plant rock star, lived on Third Street, next door to the Hell's Angels. It was always scary to see the Angels roar through the streets, and I ducked when I heard them coming, but they didn't seem to interfere with the neighbors. Gentle Rando hailed from Chicago, always covered his head with a scarf or hat, and only wore black. Neat and clean, never scruffy, he was a fitness buff before it was fashionable and possessed the air of an upright, really decent, likeable marine. I always felt safe with him because he was strong and sensible. He said he'd rather not eat and spend all his money on taxis than have to take the subway. It took me a while to figure that out, but eventually I understood.

A scrawny, red-haired drug dealer who supplied dope to Johnny Thunders liked me, lucky me. I met him at Max's. Every time I turned around, there he was, trying to look casual with his hands deep in his too-large purple tuxedo jacket. Inch by inch, step by step, smarmy Red crept closer for the kill. I thought he was strange and old, but I was too immature to know how to handle him. Red had designs and tried latching on. "Hiya, baby doll. Let me get you a drink." He slid into my booth. I kept talking to Jill and Kris, hoping he'd leave and no one would see him with us, with me. Underneath the table, he shuffled around, wrapped up, and prepared for a fix. The apparatus caught my attention; I couldn't believe it. I was astonished, shocked. How could he do that? There?

Next to *me*? I sallied from my seat as if poked with a spike, but he wasn't deterred and seemed to crawl out of dark corners all night. "Hiya, baby."

After Max's, my sisters and I headed to a popular twenty-four-hour downtown coffee shop by the tunnel. Out of the corner of my eye, I saw the purple coat when Red strolled in. Once again, he insisted on joining us at the table. "Let me buy you dolls donuts." We didn't eat donuts. He brought over his coffee and poured half a canister of sugar into his cup. "Hey, girls, I'm over in Jersey once in a while. Give me your number, and we can get together. Ride down to the shore." He leered at me and moved on in.

My sister Kris, a lot smarter than me, simply said, "No, Red." Still undeterred, he tried to impress me with a story about his father being friends with the millionaire publisher Malcolm Forbes. I was unfamiliar with the Forbes name back then, so his tale didn't get him very far, but I politely listened and started to gobble it up. Kris had had enough and said, "Get lost, Red."

Nothing ventured, nothing gained; he moved on to the next booth. We left without the donuts and without hearing the end of the story. The next morning, I did, however, mention the Forbes story to my mother, and she, being an active Republican, filled me in. Needless to say, Red's line of work wasn't mentioned. Once in a while, I saw him hanging around and he tried, tried again. "Hiya, doll. How 'bout a donut? Let's get coffee." I didn't drink coffee.

A powerful guardian angel must have watched over us

during those years, probably sent by my mother's desperate prayers. Jill and I were mostly innocent, and that seemed to create an aura around us. Like summer light, we drew insects. I drew the strangest of the species. Our exterior was black-leather clad, but inside we were pretty much sugar-and-spice, soft, sweet, giggly, girly girls, two winsome lilies dressed in black, sneering at the camera. We were so grown-up, so big, so ready to take on the world, that we cut the hair on our Barbie dolls into Debbie Harry-styled bobs and clad them in vinyl mini-dresses.

Occasionally, Kris would drive us to New York, and that made life easier. By then, the marriage to the musician was over and she loved New York and loved us, so she didn't mind. A gangly fellow named Dave hung around outside Max's. Maybe he didn't have the money to go inside to see the bands. He wore an odd type of leather spacesuit with pads at the knees. It was out of this world. Dave's sensational appearance caused Kris to drive us around the block to take a second, and then third, look while we shrieked and collapsed in laughs that continued all the way home and into the years. If I ever want Kris or Jill to laugh, all I need to say is, "Remember that guy Dave from Max's?"

In a scene in *The Doors*, Ray Manzarek suggests going to Max's for a bite to eat and then says, "These people are vampires." He was right. That scene takes place at a party at Andy Warhol's studio, the Factory, where the artist is surrounded by a group of admirers in a back room. Andy made a cameo in our lives, too. In her rock 'n' roll career, Jill dated

a Ronnie who worked for Andy Warhol. Super-nice Ronnie
lived in a great book-lined apartment on Bank Street and took
Jill to interesting but boring poetry readings and events at art
museums. She had a date with him, Andy, and Chris Stein
from Blondie. "Jill's going out with Andy Warhol tonight,"
my mother mentioned casually, as if it was something that
happened all the time. She might as well have said, *Jill's going
to the moon*, or *Jill's sailing solo around Cape Horn*, but no,
she said, "Jill's going out to dinner with Andy Warhol." What?
Why hadn't she told me? As it slowly sank in, I thought, Can
I go, too? But, I wasn't included, and we had a ferocious row.
Jill was right, of course. I hadn't been invited. However, this
would have been a chance to meet the most famous twenti-
eth-century American artist, perhaps the most influential artist
of the second half of the twentieth century, Picasso being the
first half.

I desperately wanted, needed, to go. After all, I was the
artist in the family. "I always take you everyplace with me!"
I whined, and worked myself up into a huff.

"No," she said, and shook her head. "You can't come."

"Why?"

"You weren't invited?"

"Can't you ask if I can come?"

"No!"

"Why not?" I asked.

"Because I can't."

If anything, Jill was even shyer than me, so she just could
not ask. It was not in her nature. However, I did not feel un-

derstanding about Jill's nature at the moment. I felt angry and hurt, and raised my hand and slapped her. A crushed look came upon her soft face, tears welled in the eyes, and she cried.

"Shame on you!" my mother admonished me, the wicked sister. "How could you do that?" Shamed but still wanting to go, I yelled and cried in defeat and pity for my sorry self. I had to sit that one out.

Naturally, we made up. Jill was my best friend and partner in adventure.

The coveted dinner took place at an upstairs, not very nice, dirty Chinese restaurant with lots of neon signs on Forty-second Street. The pale, ghostly Andy, skeletally thin, didn't smile or say much at all. Jill thought his hair frightfully bad, but it was actually a wig, a crazy, awful wig, and he wore eyeglasses. Andy didn't say a word to Jill, and, of course, being so shy, Jill didn't say a word to him. She felt tolerated as Ronnie's date. But Andy didn't speak to anyone else at the table, either. Ronnie ordered food family style, and it stayed in the center of the table. Poor Jill sipped rum-and-Coke and a little beer to wash away the scary monsters. Walter Steding, a Warhol painting assistant came, too. He was some sort of new-wave violinist who rode a bike all over the city. Jill said, "They were frightening and weird. It was like no one at the table existed, though we were all right in each other's faces." The young, eighteen-year-old Jill sat quietly and bored throughout the meal. (Ronnie had a long-term relationship with Debbie Harry pre-Chris Stein, so he was a man about town. I barely knew him. He was almost twenty years older than little Jill. Basically, Jill was dating Debbie's ex.)

Jill went to the Factory, too, with Bianca Jagger, Pat Cleveland, and others she doesn't remember. It was a fairly large loft space with small, scattered rooms, messy with stuff strewn about. An armed guard sat outside the Factory door on Union Square because of a previous attempt on Andy's life by an unhinged radical feminist who had shot him in the chest. She'd sought Andy's help in getting her anti-men manifesto published (such are the frustrations for an unknown trying to get published). On the studio floor lay a huge canvas, and men (and maybe women) urinated on it to oxidize the paint. Ronnie took Polaroids of Jill wearing jeans, a pink wraparound shirt, and pink sandals but kept the photos for himself. I have photos of the sandals, but no photos of the Factory, because I wasn't there. (Later, when Andy died after a routine gall bladder operation, Jill's husband's cousin would be one of the attorneys representing Warhol's estate in the wrongful death suit against the hospital.) Oddly, or maybe not so based on his humble Pennsylvania, Byzantine Catholic roots, Mr. Warhola's elderly mother lived with him in New York when he reigned as King of the Factory world. Andy impressed Jill as a Norman Bates *Psycho-* type character.

Leave it to little Jill to hit things squarely on the nose. Andy was one strange customer. From his childhood days of poverty in the Eastern European village of Pittsburgh, to his great talent and success as a commercial illustrator, to his years of rejection and then more great success as the oh-so-famous soup cans pop star, to the silkscreens of Marilyn, Liz,

Jackie, and Elvis, to the Brillo boxes to the bizarre, dark silver Factory world of misfit drag queens and rich socialites and film and Velvet Underground and the assassination attempt and the celebrity paintings, he sure was a strange angelic and demonic presence, but he certainly knew how to make piles of money, while poor mad genius of swirls and amazing color Vincent van Gogh sold only one painting during his sad life time, one more than I did. So Andy is the man I didn't meet. We probably would have gotten on just fine. The strange ones usually took a shine to me.

After the noise between us ceased, Jill generously gave me a black Andy Warhol *Interview* T-shirt that Ronnie had given her. It was my most prized possession. The sleeves were decorated with colored rhinestones. I lived in that shirt for the longest time, until it just couldn't be worn any longer. There's a picture of us cuddled together in front of a pink stucco house in the West Village. Jill wears white with a red ribbon in her hair, and I'm wearing the T-shirt and black Capris.

Andy's presence caused a ripple of excitement at a Talking Heads concert, too. As Jill and I walked along Second Avenue, someone we didn't know handed us tickets to the show. That type of thing happened to us often. Sure, why not? Let's go see the Talking Heads. When Andy entered the small, brightly illuminated concert hall, everyone turned to see the famous silvery wig, the highlight of the show. Disappointingly, it turned out to be one of the most boring concerts I ever saw, and we left before it ended.

As for Blondie, Jill and I felt kin to Debbie Harry. We

were girls from New Jersey who escaped to New York. We liked rock 'n' roll and CBGB and Max's, shared a similar style, and sometimes traveled in similar circles, but we never met her. Jill and I ambled on the deserted Asbury Park boardwalk on a brisk spring Sunday afternoon to look at the sad old carousel and disrepair of the place. (As little girls, Asbury Park dazzled us. Photos captured our gleeful faces as we rang the bell on a miniature boat ride.) We left the crumbling casino; heading toward us were two of Blondie's black-leather-clad musicians, the drummer Clem Burke and another. We were black-leather clad, too. They nodded. We smiled and thought, Wow. It was rare to see another person on a chilly spring day on the Asbury boardwalk in the 1970s, but to see two black-leather-clad girls was unusual, indeed, so they had to ask themselves, "Who are they?" We were, of course, The Cream Puffs. We only received a frosty nod of recognition in the crisp ocean air, with the blue Atlantic waves timelessly breaking in the background.

Wearing a blonde wig and superb makeup, I had a friend dress me as Debbie Harry for a party. She did a fantastic job, but those wonderful pictures are long gone. Twenty years later, sensational Debbie Harry performed with the Jazz Passengers at the Bottom Line. She appeared delicate and sweet on stage, her voice suited to jazz, but Debbie Harry will always be Blondie, much to her chagrin, I'm sure. Blondie certainly made it out of CBGB and onto the charts and television commercials. Listen to top of the pops stations; their hits are played over and over all day long.

I succumbed to blondeness, too, for a few weeks. A not very competent hairdresser named Andrew convinced me to bleach my natural black hair platinum. The strip-and-dye process lasted seven hours. The event took place at our friend Francois's oh-so-trendy shop on Prince Street. The salon was closed, but he allowed us to use it that cold Sunday. At first it was exciting anticipating this big change. Halfway through, I realized there was no turning back. The chemicals on the hair took on a smell of their own; hair no longer smelled like hair. It smelled bad, toxic. And the texture was turning to porous mush, like spaghetti that has boiled too long and starts to disintegrate in the pot. I touched it and knew my soft shiny hair was gone. When the hair dried, it was hair no more. It was lifeless stuff that had to be conditioned and coaxed and sprayed and manipulated into shape by an expert. The so-called expert had created that pulpy mess.

Afterward, we took photos, and I looked like a bona fide movie star of the Kim Novak–Marilyn variety, but it wasn't worth it, and it proved dangerous being so blonde. Passers-by yelled things, mostly original stuff like, "Whoa, Blondie!" A well-dressed businessman followed me on the street and then offered me a job as a receptionist at a chic shop. I was used to wolf-whistles and on-street attention, but this un-nerved me. Within days, the blonde hair started to break, and to my dismay, I had to cut it short into an Edie Sedgwick style with black roots and blonde tips like a German shepherd. The dyed hair felt brittle, and I hated having my face so exposed minus the long silky locks, but I soon had to cut it even shorter, to a Jean Seberg *Breathless*-style. I felt so shorn, so naked. I might as well have worn no clothes. I felt like a monkey, poor little Curious George, naked, out on a limb. Perhaps the hair symbolized other things: shiny, healthy, virgin hair, abused and then broken.

My family ignored my blonde transformation. Mother thought bleached hair epitomized a "fast," "cheap" woman. Not a word was spoken, but after I cut it off, Mom said, "Oh, you looked nice as a blonde." But even before and then during and then after—many years after—the platinum blonde hair, people would tell me I looked like Blondie, which made me laugh because I had brown eyes and black hair, but I didn't mind being told I looked like her.

Patti Smith emerged a bird of a different feather, but I felt a bond with her, too. She, also, had been raised in New Jersey, liked art and poetry and rock 'n' roll, and was smart and interesting. Jill and I came upon her on a beautiful Sunday afternoon. She was standing at One Fifth Avenue, in front of the expensive apartment building where her friend lived and the cover of *Horses* was photographed. There dwelled the downtown poet laureate and rockster. "Hey, great pants," she said to me in her unique voice. Jill and I giggled, and I was in my glory. The pants were black with little white dots, tight and short, a thrift store find, altered to fit. I didn't feel shy with her, just elated, and we exchanged a few words. After that encounter, we hung up a framed photo of an exuberant, barefoot Patti in five different dance positions, in one of which she's playing air guitar. On the same wall hung a *Wet* magazine cover featuring Debbie Harry in cowboy gear, pointing a pistol, and next to that is a painting of a classical ballerina in tutu tying her *pointe* shoes. I fancied myself rather as a hybrid of both Debbie and Patti, though I had my own style—and could look like either. I liked Debbie's "let's play dress-up" approach to fashion and Patti's unadorned self. I really was more of the latter, but in those young days, I tried to keep up with Jill, who was definitely glamorous.

I probably met Patti's guitarist Lenny Kaye at Max's; Jill said he was always there. Lenny had once worked at a record store on Bleecker Street—we would go there often—but that had probably been years before. The meeting with Patti remains more memorable. I told Lenny about the encounter and bubbled enthusiastically. I was quite inspired about Patti Smith. Lenny was tall, thoughtful, and intelligent, and patiently listened as I giggled my way through the great story of the meeting with Patti and her wonderful compliment. Over a little time and more trips to Max's, one thing led to another, and we had a date. He showed me his record albums. Gold? Platinum? Did I imagine it as the classic scenario, come up, little goose, and I'll show you my gold records? I don't know. He was a kind young man, and for once, I used the brains in my head. I didn't want a possible one-night stand. "I'm interested in a real boyfriend," I said.

"Still waters run deep," he said, sweetly agreeable and respectfully.

A postcard sent from Düsseldorf states, *I'll cross the Rar-*

itan, if you'll cross the Rhine....Maybe on a barge? xxx Lenny
Ah, the poetry of a rock 'n' roll minstrel, made all the more
delightful coming from across the ocean: He was thinking of
me. As a teenager, Lenny lived in New Brunswick, the Hub
City; I was from Perth Amboy, the Bay City, Middlesex
County, New Jersey. The Raritan River runs from New
Brunswick to Perth Amboy. The barge refers to a bad restaurant. Patti Smith was raised in South Jersey. Debbie Harry
came from North Jersey, and I grew up in Central. We were
three unlikely representatives of the Garden State, three unlikely tenders of produce.

Lenny liked me or liked writing. Recently, another old
postcard turned up in a box of photographs. The card is from
Venice and dated September 16. The year is unclear, maybe
it's 1978 or 1979. *Why does sitting by the Grand Canal here
remind me of the river that crosses New Jersey and Staten Island? Got me...hope all is well with you. Love, Lenny*, he
wrote from far- away, enchanting Venice, and signed off with
amore, and my head was in the clouds.

New Brunswick is home to Rutgers University, the State
University of New Jersey, where Lenny Kaye graduated and
later went on to teach a popular class. Jill hosted a live radio
show at Rutgers for a short time, where she played the "New
Wave" of music. Young high-school teenager Jill got that spot
by talking to someone at a party. We had all the latest imports
from the U.K., so Jill starred with her records as a guest DJ
on Saturday nights. She invited a Joey Poole and Franché
(pronounced Frankie), someone from a band called the Mis-

fits, as performers, live on the air. We had met these two crazy but friendly Misfits at CBGB, where they downed beer, beer after beer, in the car on the way to New Brunswick, laughing and talking and banging the dashboard like Gene Krupa. Most of their conversation revolved around music and their buddy, a certain drummer named Marc Bell. In classic North Jersey parlance, Lodi speak, they pronounced Marc "Mock" or "Mock-ee." They were big fans of Mock. Mock-ee this and Mock-ee that, everyone liked Marc. By the time we reached Rutgers, Joey and Franché were raring to go, and one of those two North Jersey bad boys said something inappropriate that began with "f" live on the Rutgers University radio station. That was the end of young Jill's DJ stint, but she didn't care. Saturday night was club night, so the radio show put a crimp in our schedule.

About the same time, Marc Bell, the Ramones' new drummer, invited us, Jill and me, to see them perform at some club on the outskirts of New Brunswick. Backstage, we ran into an old girlfriend of old friend Jesus de Jesus, a reporter for the Rutgers newspaper. "Good to see you! What are you doing here?" she asked.

"Oh, I'm with Marc," I replied and smiled.

Hearing the Ramones for the first time shocked, like being slammed into a wall of high voltage electricity and having the soles blown off your feet. It was a big clap of thunder and crack of lightning, followed by a flash freeze. Visually, the four guys in black leather jackets in a small space sent another jolt. No one laughed; no one smiled. "One, two, three, four!"

I felt electrocuted but still breathing, as if I had cheated death. None of those sensations ever diminished. I had been knocked down by a wave of sound, fallen into a pool of crystal-clear icy water, and emerged, safe but still wet and ready for the warmth and protection of my own heavy black leather jacket.

Back at Max's, Cheetah Chrome, from the brash band the Dead Boys, chased me around while his scary wife Gyda Gash hunkered by. "C'mere, Beauty," he growled, ready to paw me. (It wasn't until I read *Visions of Cody* thirty years later that I understood the meaning of Gyda's surname, and thirty years later, the Dead Boys sound pretty good: ferocious dogs barking, gun shots, police sirens.) I didn't care for the attentions of Mr. Chrome from Cleveland—that strange agent of the night—he was definitely someone to run away from. Listen to the Dead Boys' (another charming name) "Son of Sam" and imagine being pursued by one of them. I wanted no encounter with Mrs. Chrome either. She looked like she could eat me alive, and I didn't need that. Chrome sported bright orange hair and printed tights, chains, and a dog collar—not for me. No, thanks.

Jill had strange luck that same night. The short one from Hall and Oates robustly chased her in the dark nooks and crannies of Max's and tried to phone afterward. She didn't like him, and we had a lot of fun at little Pepe La Pu's expense.

A photographer and professor of film study we knew said that Jill had a perfectly symmetrical face. That, and her soft, wavy hair and super fashion sense, caused her quite a bit of chase and run. On New York City streets, people stopped to stare at her. She was always as sparkling clean and fresh, as if she had just alighted from a shower.

> *Angels and ministers of grace defend us.*
> *Be thou a spirit of health, or goblin damned,*
> *Bring with thee airs from heaven, or blasts from hell,*
> *Be thy intents wicked, or charitable,*
> *Thou com'st in such a questionable shape,*
> *That I will speak to thee*
>
> —Hamlet

4

LOVE NEW YORK

❧

AT JILL'S HIGH SCHOOL GRADUATION, I wore black spandex pants recently bought from Fiorucci's in Hollywood, a French T-shirt with a huge drawing of a French pop star covering the front—given to me by a record promoter—and black patent-leather stilettos from Ian's, a pricey New York City boutique that specialized in clothes imported from London. A lovely English rose of a girl worked there. She was slender and curvy, with creamy English skin. Her blonde hair was tied up on top of her head in a messy nest. She was Johnny Thunders's or Jerry Nolan's girlfriend, or maybe she was someone's sister, but she was someone, that girl—a real Brit bird, with great big Tweety Bird blue eyes.

In the spring of 1979, I had gone to California with Marc, now Marky Ramone, when they were recording *End of the Century*. My clothes presented a great embarrassment to my chagrined parents; stoically they accepted what they could not

change, which was me during the height of my rebellion, and
my aberrant appearance caused a stir in the crowded bleach-
ers. Rows of heads turned to catch a glimpse of this apparition. If any of my former teachers saw me, so be it. They
should look so good.

A lightning bolt struck Jill's classmate, Daniel, when he
saw this rock 'n' roll creature in his midst, and from that moment on he was devoted to us and our quest for life in the big
city. We were an inseparable team of three. Jill and I didn't
drive, but Daniel did, and he was more than willing to take
us anyplace at any time. We changed Daniel's life, and he im-
proved ours. He showered us with his time and gifts: beautiful
party dresses with pouf skirts, quality costume jewelry from
flea markets, and records that he painstakingly selected. We
didn't like the poufs much, Daniel's taste wasn't our taste, but
not wanting to hurt his feelings, we thanked him, wore them
once or twice, and then gave them away. Daniel was proud
of his finds, but they took up valuable closet space. The
dresses probably came from the 1950s or 1960s, and neither
Jill nor I wanted to look that way. Looking sultry, like Nico,
the model, singer, songwriter, Andy Warhol superstar, and the
Velvet Underground's own, was closer to our ideal. We tried
to discourage Daniel from shopping sprees, but the dresses
kept coming, as did the piles of earrings, necklaces, and
brooches. He shopped with a passion and got to go with two
beautiful girls to the places where we went. Daniel denied
being homosexual, but we didn't care what he was; we loved
him and had fun together. Short and stocky, he wasn't hand-

some, but he had style, a big black pompadour, and a gift for socializing. We went to the clubs, and Daniel drank in the heady atmosphere. He was a natural lounge lizard and loved the exhilaration, the sights and sounds, and knew how to schmooze and advance up the social ladder. He had an innate ability to know whom to avoid as well, and he danced and moved with ease.

I, who didn't drive, had to drive us all home to New Jersey late one night because Daniel had drunk too much. At that time in the wee hours on a Sunday morning, there were almost no other cars on the turnpike. My only fear was getting through the Holland Tunnel without running the car into the tiled walls; after that it was easy: Just go straight. It beat taking the bus. On the New Jersey Turnpike, passing the oil refineries, brightly, eerily lit chemical works, and pipelines with giant clouds of smoke and gases being discharged into the air looked not unlike a ghastly modern Hieronymus Bosch. I didn't mind. We were almost home. "Hold back the edges of your gowns, ladies," wrote fellow New Jerseyan William Carlos Williams, "we are going through hell." Apparently, he had taken the same drive. Soon, we took off the high heels and tight evening clothes and settled in our own little angelic beds—safe, home sweet home.

Daniel was shrewd, manipulative, smart, and funny. He inspired loyalty in people and for a long time worked at a liquor store where he stole enough booze to keep East Village parties and poetry readings going and somehow managed to keep his job while he attended cosmetology school. He had a

clear, focused criminal mind, the mind of a crafty politician
or successful entrepreneur. He bribed people with stolen alcohol; at the top of the list were doormen at downtown clubs.
We never paid to get into clubs. In fact, the doorkeepers were
always happy to see us and let down the rope for our entrance.
For a time, Daniel might have been selling Quaaludes, too,
but I never officially knew that. I did, however, have a closet
stocked with gallons of vodka that came in handy when I had
bribes of my own to make, as when I bought a small but heavy
table on Elizabeth Street and couldn't get a cab to take it
home. A Bowery man helped me lift and carry it all the way
to East Fifth Street, and he was thusly rewarded.

The apartment came via a real estate agency. The rotund
agent lived in a huge, comfortable Chelsea townhouse with
fireplaces, and a nice big dog gently moved from room to
room. The little East Fifth Street place could fit in her bathroom, and I resented paying the hefty fee. However, a tiny
apartment in the East Village is better than no apartment.
New York was my Paris, a city of light and much more, the
only place I ever really wanted to live. A small, secure Manhattan apartment would mean more to me than a giant mansion anyplace in the world. For the moment, the tiny,
not-at-all-secure, one-lock-on-the door East Village flat would
have to do, and it did.

At home in Perth Amboy, our windows faced the Arthur
Kill and onto bucolic Tottenville, Staten Island—the southern-
most tip of New York City. New York, literally, was in our
backyard, and it turned out to be our playground.

Halloween is big time in the Village. At night, an amazing parade that started as a community event with costumes ranging from 101 Dalmatians to spurned political figures accompanies extravagantly undressed samba bands. A good time is guaranteed on a soft October night. Before I lived on East Fifth, my father would take us to the parade. He loved New York and had passed it on to us. My father brought us to the city at least once a week. When we were younger, we ventured to Mulberry Street via the Staten Island ferry or drove to the Central Park Zoo or American Museum of Natural History. Awesome to a little girl rose the classical architecture of old New York, majestic buildings of granite, limestone, and marble, and columns, cornices, and staircases leading to grand entrances; and the bronze equestrian statues that graced parks and public squares; and the marble lions of The New York Public Library. Prized was an annual trip to the Bronx Zoo, followed by shopping for specialty foods on Arthur Avenue, where we would stop for clams on the half shell. As young adults, we delighted in the St. Francis Day procession of the blessing of the animals at the Cathedral of St. John the Divine. The giant cathedral welcomed an elephant, camel, llamas, and dogs of all sizes.

The extravagant 1964 *Ice Capades* at Madison Square Garden is a cherished memory from early childhood, captured in a photo from that glorious adventure. Seated next to me on the couch is a black teddy bear on skates. Riding on the fast train into Pennsylvania Station excited my young imagination; if it had been the Orient Express, it couldn't have been

grander. I took pleasure in the passing scenery and the large-
ness of the train station and the arena and the bustle of the
passers-by, and delighted in the skaters and their costumes and
the ice skating rink still frozen in summertime. The marvelous
event came to an end, and waiting in the grand concourse of
the station, I bought my sister a grainy black-and-white Beatles magazine and looked at it on the way home.

In the year 1964, my father took us to see the new Ver-
razano-Narrows Bridge that connected Brooklyn and Staten
Island. I hid under the car seat and cried the first time we
went over it, because I remembered it as just a skeleton of en-
gineering, not the completed structure, and I was afraid the
whole family would plunge into the deep water.

Less traumatizing was our trip to Lincoln Center and seeing the shooting Revson Fountain.

Wonder of wonders loomed in the 1964 New York
World's Fair. In a hushed room, silent and dark as a cathedral,
stood Michelangelo's *Pieta*, and I knew I was seeing the sublime and beheld the holy face of the Son of God and his in-
carnate white marble flesh and the holy face and figure of His
perfect Mother. Innocent child I knew this. That a man had
created that work of art staggered me completely and absolutely. How could it be? The Michelangelo image of God
the Father touching the finger of Adam is my image of God:
the noble strong old man with the flowing white hair and
beard. I like it. God is spirit. Yes, yes, yes, but I like the shiny
hair and grand *pater*. Michelangelo's *Pieta* is my image of the
dead Christ in the arms of his serene, suffering Mother. Seeing

the work of Michelangelo was all the theology I needed.

The secular General Motors "Futurama" show for the Space Age was another out-of-this world highlight. A glimpse of the future was revealed to wide young eyes. We might be living on the moon, or in a glass bubble in Antarctica or a City of the Future, like the Jetsons. We rode through the exhibit in comfy modern chairs on a ride train. Oh, boy! *Swoosh*, seven-year-old I held hands with one of my older sisters.

Along with those new additions to the city, incredulously, the Beaux-Arts masterpiece that was Pennsylvania Station, modeled on the ancient Roman Baths of Caracalla, came under demolition in the mid-1960s, a stupidity of monumental proportions. Again, how could this be? Look at the photos of that phenomenal building and weep.

At the end of the same decade, Dad took us in the summer of 1969 to the ticker-tape parade down Broadway in lower Manhattan in honor of the Apollo 11 crew: Neil Armstrong, Buzz Aldrin, and Michael Collins, the first men to set foot upon the moon. At the time, it was the largest parade in history. As a twelve-year-old, it was fantastic and very, very exciting being part of the crowd, being part of history, and being showered by, and walking on, a thick carpet of ticker tape. That summer remained a summer of joyful innocence before the competitor and her marijuana cigarette, before the hateful cafeteria fight, before the schism between my mother and Kris, before Mills the predatory beast, and before my uncle's violent death—innocent days *Before the Revolution,* in the care of my parents and surrounded by my siblings and seeing the men who had walked on the moon.

Downtown stayed a special place. Crisp-skinned ducks hung in shop windows, multitudes of strange fishes in plastic buckets neatly lined vendors' stalls, and the crowds and smells of Chinatown fascinated. The cafes of Little Italy, with glass cases of tempting pastries, the aroma of strong coffee and the round, sharp-smelling cheeses and meats suspended from salumeria ceilings, and displays of big loaves, were wonderful. Early in the morning, we went to the Fulton Street Fish Market among the trucks and shouts of the workingmen and cases packed with ice and slippery, silvery sea creatures. Bearded, sandaled beatniks in Washington Square Park frightened me as a child, but they held my fascination. When we drove through the Bowery, my father said, "Make sure the doors are locked," but he rolled down his window and handed the unkempt stranger attempting to wash the windshield a discreet bill. "That man could be anyone. He could have been a doctor or judge or a stockbroker." It was hard to comprehend that about the gray man on the street. My father always gave the down-and-outs money, and he always gave waiters big tips.

In green Central Park surrounded by tall buildings, the pedigree dogs of pedigree Fifth Avenue residents paraded past. We fed the squirrels and pigeons and had a picnic lunch. The zoo animals looked miserable in their bare concrete city cages, before the zoo's renovation. Smooth sleek seals swam round and round, and we played at the old Children's Zoo with the smiling whale and Noah's Ark.

Later, when Kris attended Finch College, it was a treat to visit her at the townhouse on East Seventy-second Street between Fifth and Madison and was indeed an extra bonus to stay in her dorm for the weekend. The student body there all seemed to be beautiful, elegant girls with lovely long hair and silky skin. Each polite and well-spoken young woman seemed to have stepped out of a fashion magazine. They spent weekends shopping on Madison Avenue or going to the glorious Frick Collection after Sunday brunch. The Village and its environs were off limits to the girls. White-gloved, uniformed attendants served the students in the dining room. As we matured, we dined and delighted in midtown Lutèce and La Grenouille, but downtown had a hold on my young heart. The desirable Edith Wharton, historic, charming West Village, was too pricey, so I settled for what I could afford, the seedy East, covered in grime and dereliction.

Jill, Daniel, their friends—fashionable Suzy who went to Fashion Institute and a blonde, unassuming, not terribly ambitious second Jill—spent time at my tiny apartment. On weekends, three or four might sleep under the loft, and once in a while their friends would stay, too. After clubbing on Saturday night, Daniel would cook ham and eggs on English muffins or take us to breakfast, where we discussed the previous night's juicy events, who'd worn what, whom we'd met, and then we might go to the movies on St. Mark's Place or to a flea market or to the antique shops in the West Village.

Often, Jill and Daniel would stay out too late for me. I couldn't always keep up with them, and head home earlier

and regret it the next day when they discussed the night's offering.

"What happened?" I asked knowing it was a treat I'd
missed.

"We ran into a drunken Truman Capote having coffee,"
Jill said laughing.

"He was short, *so* short," Daniel added. Daniel was
short, too. "And, drunk, *so* drunk." Knowing Daniel, he'd
probably been somewhat drunk as well. They quieted down
for a moment. "And," Daniel said on the verge of hysterics,
"he talked like this." He launched into a Tru impersonation.

"Where did you see him? Who was he with? What was
he wearing? How did you know he was drunk? Did you say
anything to him?" I asked, greatly intrigued.

Holly Golightly, as Capote wrote of her, "was such a sym-
bol of all these girls who come to New York and spin in the
sun for a moment like May flies and then disappear." May
fly, I?

A friend named Richard wrote for the *East Village Eye*.
He had graduated from a Boston college and was a snob. He
wrote poetry, and his best piece was about a donkey. On a
bright sunny Sunday, on top of a Bowery rooftop, Richard
read his poem and brayed, a proper Bostonian ass. The crowd
all had Bloody Marys in hand, thanks to Daniel, and a Bowery
resident looked on with interest from a neighboring roof. It
felt good to be young and alive and on top of the world on a
rooftop on the island of Manhattan, surrounded by friends

mellow with drink and the beautiful day.

Richard Smith's personal sense of style was rare for downtown, simple and straightforward. He had beautiful, wavy brown hair and always wore the same outfit: a polo or oxford shirt, and straight jeans. Sometimes, he wore light bucks. He was the only one downtown dressing that way; thus he proved the most original of all. He lived in an apartment as small as mine but with a bathtub in the center of the room. Richard said the only good thing about my apartment was that it was on the second floor, so there weren't that many stairs to climb. He was blunt in his criticisms and free with comments about what he perceived as our lack of education, which made me uneasy. On the wall of his apartment was a photo of cowboy Clint Eastwood. One late afternoon, out of loneliness, I went to see Richard; he was frying potatoes in a pan for dinner, the only food he had. A chubby, un-hip Boston friend was sitting at his table. Uncomfortable being there, I didn't stay long.

Even though Richard claimed he loathed rock 'n' roll and said musicians should only be allowed to enter a place via the kitchen and should be treated as servants, it seemed he always got the first job at every new club in town: midtown Bonds where we had the best time dancing to James Brown, Danceteria, Area, Hurrah, and World. In all those clubs, including CBGB and Max's, there were no fights, no guns, and no such thing as metal detectors. One or two burly bouncers sufficed. Raw, unadorned CBGB was the most innocent of the clubs, maybe because the patrons were so young, maybe because we were so young. After CBGB and Max's and the Mudd Club, the later clubs all blurred together, and I couldn't distinguish one from the other. When Danceteria opened, it kept being shut down. Every Saturday night, the FDNY would march in, and the fire marshals would turn on the lights and send everyone home. Exposed in the light, the partygoers looked more garish than attractive, and Richard no longer seemed so sure of himself next to the brawny, fresh-faced firefighters. It seemed the best-looking guys in New York were the young Irish firemen.

I never dated a fireman, but I did spend a short evening with a police officer once. He was huge and had worked as Nelson Rockefeller's bodyguard. Officer McKenna came over, and I offered him a whisky, courtesy of Daniel, of course. He was kind but frightened me, I disliked the gun, and we had nothing in common. I felt awkward and, thankfully, he stayed briefly. However, it was good to know him. One night with Daniel behind the wheel, Richard, Jill, blonde Jill, Suzy, me, and whoever else could fit in that car, were stopped not too far from home in the Ninth Precinct. "Oh, no!" Daniel moaned when he saw the flashing lights of the patrol car behind him.

"Don't worry, I'll take care of this," I said. ". . .Hi, Officer." I smiled as I crawled over the bodies, rolled down the car window, and addressed the young cop. "We're just going down the street. Oh, Bob McKenna's a friend."

He let us go. There, Richard, I said to my prideful self, you're not the only one with pull.

Daniel became Richard's bosom pal, so Richard's clubs

continually opened to us like an oyster, with the liquor as the pearl, but I grew tired of going out after midnight, tired of dressing up, painting my face, thinking of original clothes to wear, being the first to have the best shoes or handbag, and figuring out how to afford it. Slowly my interest in the clubs waned. I was bored with the hip artists and musicians, everyone trying to outdo each other and, therefore, all looking and acting the same. Wary of the posturing and posing, I was slowly, very slowly, growing up. Tight-pants Andrew was a friend we would all grow to dislike—but Richard loathed him straight off and went out of his way to humiliate him. Richard allowed Jill, Daniel, and me into the clubs but demanded that the accompanying Andrew pay. It was then that I noticed Richard resembled a bulldog.

Sometimes Jill would get into tiffs with Daniel. He especially hated Jill's Andy Warhol friend Ronnie, because he was odd man out when Ronnie was in. Sophisticated Ronnie was a little too much competition for jealous Danny boy. Daniel tucked his head into his shirt like a hard little turtle and didn't come out until Ronnie left.

Daniel only wanted to be with the most chic people and would select a trendy guy at a club for Jill, so that he could hang out with him. Jill, though, had her own mind and wasn't going to do it. One of Daniel's chosen was Bark, a tough, red-haired hairdresser from Detroit. Bark had a neat little apartment where a huge naked black man with long dreadlocks spent a lot of time. Daniel didn't know about the naked Jamaican. He went to Bark's apartment and In-the-Buff opened the door. Expecting Bark, Daniel nearly died. After that, things went well for the three, on occasion, four, but then Bark's drinking got the best of him, the friendship soured, and that was pretty much the end of Bark—except that he tried one last, unsuccessful time to get back into the fold. Wearing a full face of Baby Jane Hudson makeup, he followed Jill to Macy's. He rode up and down the escalator behind her, trying to get her attention. Cool and sweet as a strawberry ice-cream cone, she froze the ridiculous interloper out and swiftly, deftly, slipped out the side door. What a way to win back the girl!

Daniel liked going to an old Ukrainian bar with a great jukebox on St. Mark's Place. Old men sat there drinking Stoli until a certain hour, and then kids came in, drank Stoli, and took over. After the bar, we headed to one of the Ukrainian diner-type restaurants, a clean place on Avenue A that provided gigantic home-cooked meals with soup and yeasty braided bread for less than four dollars. Hefty Ukrainian mothers ran the place, and no one got out of line.

During one of Daniel's many flea market shopping jaunts, Jill and I tagged along; he found a hideous, circus brute Zampanò plaid men's suit. "Daniel," I asked, afraid he was going to give it to me. "What are you going to do with that?"

"This is great," he said without listening. "I'm not going to chance leaving this behind. I'll take it."

It didn't fit him, so he gave it to Andrew. The trousers and sleeves were way too short, and both garments were button-popping tight. It was a buffoon's suit, and the effect was outrageously comical. Surprisingly, the terribly vain Andrew was a good sport and tried it on. We fell on the floor laughing and carried on for a while, wiping the tears from our faces, until Andrew returned to his everyday leather pants.

"Well," Daniel acquiesced. "You might as well keep it." It would have been a good fit for louch Red, but I donated it to the Salvation Army.

When I worked as a makeup artist, my freelance assignment was to paint a young reveler into a zebra. I used Andrew as a model. He wore white tights and leotard and stood still while I sprayed black body paint on it and him, but the paint came off his skin with soap and water. It was easy to cover the young man's face with white pancake makeup and then apply black stripes. We covered his head with a white cap to which artificial black hair was attached, were pleased with the results, and he paid me a grand seventy-five dollars, my first commission.

Jill worked as a makeup artist at a snooty place on Madison Avenue in the upper 60s. Kay, the owner, was addicted to prescription drugs; she'd be high and then sink low. The shop had a pharmacy in back where her husband practiced as a pharmacist and provided the girls with drugs. When Kay hired a new girl, she handed her a broom and said, "Sweep." If you took it and swept, she treated you badly; if you stood up to her and said, "I was hired as a makeup artist," she respected you. Jill was warned about Kay, so she had the inside scoop. Kay's problematic son hit on the new employees, and if you turned him down, he made life difficult until your demise. Jill and a co-worker approached Kay and told her. He never came on to them again but made life miserable. His nastiness was overshadowed by the shop's main attraction, the clientele, and that held the girls' interest.

Jill was a smart little cookie who seldom missed a trick and provided some of her succinct and keen observations that I can only tell and not show, because I wasn't there. Besides, maybe someday Jill will show and tell you in her own book: Carly Simon was thin with long, curly brown hair, and rude, only bought a brown eyeliner pencil. She didn't smile, not once. Simpatica, glamorous Gina Lollobrigida had a huge smile and shopped, filling a hand-held basket. Iman was beautiful and exotic in a floor-length white fur coat, professional and polite. Jeri Hall, in head-to-toe purple spandex, wore a white fur coat with leopard lining, and looked very much like a drag queen, but smiled, Texas friendly. The model Janice Dickenson was quite nasty and wore a Robin Hood outfit complete with a bag perfect for bows and arrows, while the model Beverly Johnson appeared quiet and dignified in a simple navy double-breasted wool coat. Gene Simmons and Paul Stanley of Kiss wore no makeup and were more interested in picking up the makeup artists than in buying anything except hairbrushes; both were ugly. Kirk Douglas and his wife were nice to all the girls, and Ginger Rogers, sadly, had become quite aged but still shopped for makeup. Diana Ross, sans any glamour and with a doo rag on her head, looked the complete opposite of a pop diva. Sophia Loren, the magnificent Cesira, *La Ciociara*, had a huge presence that overwhelmed the place.

Harassed and crazed Kay implored her employees to ignore the celebrities and treat them like everyone else. Instead, the staff ignored Kay, stared at the celebs good and hard, and made mental notes, so they could go home and give their friends the inside info. With me working on West Fifty-fifth Street, Daniel coiffing hair in the East Village, and pseudo-friend Andrew doing the same in Soho, we had the town covered. Daniel scoffed at the famous, and Andrew slept with them.

Those were mostly funny, happy times, and we mostly had a ball, but it would take some years before the dust settled and the personality clashes mended. Photos from those days show us laughing, sitting around with drinks in hand.

Once, Daniel took us to a big amusement park, and Jill and I went on the baby rides. The best picture shows Daniel with a genuine smile as wide as the camera, no downtown posturing in sight. We wore some of Daniel's flea-market finds. Daniel and Richard were both great dancers and amusing, and the music and dancing brought us joy and a way to celebrate our youth. On special occasions when we did celebrate a birthday or some other event, it was with a chocolate mousse cake and bottle of champagne. This was our *A Moveable Feast*. Stylish, young, and living in the greatest city on earth, we lived our life to the full, however little we actually ate.

Eventually, Daniel got an apartment with new friends on Avenue B. One of the girls had short blonde hair and wore thick black-framed glasses—not a glamour-puss. The apartment was large, but I was apprehensive about the somewhat abandoned neighborhood and only went there once. The last time I saw Daniel, when I was still living in New York, he slogged down the bright morning street nonchalantly smoking pot on his way to work, just another day. Years later, Daniel the natural wheeler-dealer, went on to become a successful business owner. That didn't surprise me. He married and had children, divorced, and remains in New York.

That their society, as their friendship, may
Be merely poison! Nothing I'll bear from thee
But nakedness, thou detestable town!
—Timon of Athens

5

MARC AND THE RAMONES,

AND A PEEK AT BURROUGHS

⌒⌒

I MET MARC ONE STICKY NIGHT at CBGB. We stood pinned next to each other with our sides touching and, eventually, turned to look at each other. The packed crowd crushed me against the wall. The noise made it too difficult to talk, but Jill discreetly pointed and loudly whispered in my ear, "He's Marc Bell." He was still Marc Bell then, and he appeared preoccupied, serious, but said hi and asked for my phone number. He was leaving Richard Hell's band to take Tommy's place as the Ramones' drummer. It sounded terribly exciting, and he was kind of cute. It might have been the last night he played with Richard Hell, so maybe that's why our introduction was so brief.

(The Ramones were one of the best bands to emerge from CBGB and would be critically acclaimed. *Rolling Stone* rated *Ramones* as number thirty-three on its list of the 500 greatest albums of all time, and they were inducted into the Rock and

Roll Hall of Fame. However, for all their influence and critical accolades, the seminal band never had a breakthrough hit during their career, though they had an enormous influence on popular music in the United States. They were more popular in the United Kingdom, Europe, South America, and Japan than they were in this country. Marc played with the Ramones for fifteen years.)

Marc started to call me right away, and after my initial shock, I liked him. He was well known in music circles and admired by his friends and peers. He turned out to be a wildly funny and original guy from Brooklyn—quite a distant place. His father was a longshoreman who became a lawyer, he said, and even that seemed funny.

I must have soon met the new band, because I surmised that Marc seemed different than the original three, who, at that point in their careers, seemed eager to get on with bigger things, and he was still treated as an outsider. It was a business to them—free-market capitalism, their job. They had been being the Ramones for a while and were ready for a breakthrough. Marc was a little more carefree and younger. I certainly was no judge, but those in the know—like our friend Brad who also played drums—pronounced Marc an accomplished drummer, and Brad looked up to him.

Watching Marc play was fun. He put his whole being into his performance. For easier arm movement, the sleeves of his T-shirts were cut off, revealing his thin but strong arms. He pounded those drums and kept going using his hands and arms and feet—one hand did one thing, the other did something else, and the high-top sneaker feet moved, too. All the while, he made the most incredibly hilarious faces that made Jill and me laugh. At home, we would imitate his movements and faces and collapse on the bed in delight.

Marc called and asked me to meet him at Max's. I was so overwhelmed, so anxious, so flushed, I almost wished he hadn't called. I took great care in finding something perfect to wear and hopped on the bus to New York alone, with my heart doing flip-flops. I took a cab to Seventeenth Street, arrived first, and sat with my friend Randolph until Marc came in with what seemed to me every one of his Brooklyn friends. I should have brought Jill, but I'd thought it was a date, one boy and one girl. After some clowning on his part and giggles on mine, he ordered a bottle of Lancer's, and that was a particularly glamorous moment. *I had arrived.* I was sitting in Max's with a very promising rock 'n' roller who seemed to like me. However, being so ultra-sensitive and so tense and worried about my parents' reaction and how I was going to get home that night and not appear like a big baby, and due to outside influences, the date was an utter disaster. Somehow, at some point, someone had given me a Quaalude, and I wasn't aware of the effects, plus I was drinking wine. Quite simply, I was, one of the few times in my life, wasted, completely, completely trashed. Rando kept an eye on me at Max's.

"Are you okay?" he asked, nice and blurry.

I was anything but okay.

"Sure, Rand. I'm fine," I replied on my way out the door

and onto oblivion.

We—Marc, his friends, and me—piled into a cab and headed to a club on West Eighth Street that had a long, narrow, dark staircase. I reached the top of those stairs but slipped, tumbled, blacked out, and ended up in Brooklyn. I rubbed my eyes and woke up to see an angry Marc peering at my face. His friends were still there, standing behind him. The apartment was brightly lit like an emergency room. "Where am I?" I mumbled most unhappily and hoped to die.

Marc insisted I stay for my own safety, but being the stubborn thing that I was and knowing what would happen if I didn't get home, I insisted on leaving. I felt ruined, my life over, but I had to get back to my parents in New Jersey. I thought I could go outside and hail a cab as I could in Manhattan. Wrong: There were no cabs on that quiet, wide, residential boulevard late at night. I somehow made it back to Manhattan. Did I actually hitchhike? No. Not even I, in all my young angst, could have been that crazy. Could I? Somehow I made it to the safety of New Jersey, and my sweet bed and soft covers, home sweet home. I pulled the covers over my disgraced head and hoped to never wake up from my self-inflicted imbroglio.

There was also the little incident of the white-handled switchblade I found, walking home from school one day, falling out of my handbag onto Marc's floor. Something like that happened. How could I remember? I kept the little knife as a prop to improve my image as a tough-as-nails, no more victim, femme fatale *Tosca*. I hoped to appear street-smart, cool. When I came to, did I leap up, unsheathe and brandish my sword—the bare bodkin—at the Brooklyn Dodgers like Tybalt? Mercutio? Romeo? Hamlet? Ah, it's entirely possible. Anything could have happened that night, anything bad, that is, but nothing good.

Oh, boy, oh, boy, how very ridiculous I was.

In the morning, waves of shame washed over me. I never, ever wanted to get out of bed or face anyone, especially Marc, for the rest of my life, but I had to undo the damage. I wanted nothing more than to sink in the soft covers and vanish. Faced with the reality that I had to get on with my ruined life, I ascended the valley of humiliation, and that afternoon, Jill and I were, once again, in New York. We ran into Brad, who had seen me in the club with the long, narrow staircase. "You were like a rag doll," he said, a drugged, sorrowful, sack of limpness, and possibly dangerous. Great. My face turned hot as I blushed a flaming red. We called Marc and met him in the West Village. He was still angry, but he softened, and the event was eventually pretty much forgotten by him but very much remembered by me. I never liked Brooklyn after that, and from that misadventure, Marc seemed many times to address me in a slightly scolding tone.

He lived in an older, spacious apartment building with a big courtyard at the entrance where old ladies sat in the Ocean Parkway sunshine. A couple of short flights of stairs led to his unit. The halls were cool. The keyhole on the front door of his apartment was big enough so you could look and see inside. Jill and I did not at all know Brooklyn. When we went there, we got totally, helplessly lost. It is such a big place, and we weren't familiar with the subways, streets, or people. A whole new environment engulfed us. Don't ask what prompted me, with poor Jill in tow, to go there one Sunday afternoon, but we did. I don't know if Marc knew we were coming, but we went. He may have been sleeping, he may have been with someone, I don't know, but through the key-hole of his front door, we could see him get up and stagger around, ignoring us ringing the bell. We giggled at the key-hole, with our hands over our mouths like cartoon characters, peering in. He appeared in his white skin, thin arms and legs, soft belly, and white underpants against the white walls of his bare apartment. We didn't say anything. I timidly knocked. He said nothing, just fumbled about and went back to bed. There was nothing to do but leave, not wanting to raise his ire again or the curiosity of the old ladies in the building. I was sorry, especially for Jill, who was a good sport, that we had made the long trip by bus and subway in our high-heeled shoes, and was embarrassed but laughed it off as absurdly funny.

Since we were in Brooklyn someplace, with Marc unavail-able, we had lunch at a kosher deli. The rude waitress couldn't understand us; we couldn't understand her—she was too fast, we weren't fast enough. "Whadda you have, goiles? I ain't got all day. Speak up." We finished our pastrami and hurried out. It was another disaster and left me rather de-flated, but I didn't want Jill to know how foolish I felt. It was-n't every day that we traveled to Brooklyn, and Jill and I never went there together again.

Far-away Brooklyn and that apartment just didn't click. It just wasn't meant to be. I should have given up right then. However, a pleasant memory remains of listening to a Helen Reddy record there, "Ain't No Way to Treat a Lady," and admiring her lovely voice. Marc played it over and over again. When it finished playing, he got up and played it again, and again. It seemed an unusual song for a Ramone to like. I hadn't heard it in years, but when I did again, it brought back that sunny, muggy afternoon and I smiled. Another record Marc played repeatedly—I'd never heard it before and haven't since—started off with clown music. The first line was, "Good-bye, cruel world, I'm off to join the circus. . . ." That was fitting, and he did indeed join a circus of sorts.

Marc took me to dinner that day at an empty restaurant, and he ordered wine in a grown-up way, like my father. We talked little, and I hardly ate. If I was twenty, he was twenty-five, but both Jill and I thought he was older. He must have liked me a little but never said so. I gave him the floor, and he said funny things and made funny faces, and I laughed but said not a word.

Marc was intelligent and popular and had many friends, many friends from Brooklyn, guys and girls. He also had two women friends. They were both very, very scary, with stony, mean faces. Of course, neither of them wanted me around. They both might have been there that first night at CBGB. One was six feet tall and thin, with strawberry-blonde hair parted on the side, squinty eyes, deadly pale skin, and a deep voice. Her face seemed capable of only one expression, displeasure, and her body was ramrod straight and void of movement. Being that I was an arbiter of fashion, I judged her open-collared shirt, straight black skirt, and low-heeled shoes a scream, when in reality she had simple good taste and the pluck to demonstrate it in the midst of spandex and leopard print.

The other friend was a scruffy-jeans-and-T-shirt girl with dirty feet. She was very thin but with a bosom and had the trashy look I'd once tried to imitate. That look was neglect. She had been with Red the drug dealer and Johnny Thunders in that Canal Street walkup, and was probably a user. I didn't ask any questions and didn't get any answers. I was uncomfortably out of my league and, many years later, had a suspicion that the trashy one may have been a prostitute, but I may have been wrong. Old friend Brad called her a "pros." I didn't know what that meant and, of course, didn't ask, because I felt I had to appear sophisticated, but one day the meaning went off in my head like a light bulb. Wow. Imagine that, but I couldn't really imagine that. It was too far-fetched. How could a girl, a thin, young girl like me, do that? Why? Where? When? How often? Did Marc know? Did she give him money? The questions stayed in my head.

For the little I knew, the strawberry-blonde might have been a librarian. She looked older, but probably wasn't; she was probably just mature. I referred to her as the Barbie doll, which Jill and I found deliciously clever. "Why do you call her that?" Marc chided. "You look more like a Barbie doll than she does." I wasn't six feet tall, but I kept that to myself. Marc was bolder than I, more confident, and had the upper hand. He also had the apartment and the cool job. I was a not as assertive Layla to his *Buffalo 66* Billy Brown.

There were good, funny times with Marc and some not so funny times. We went to Music Row on Forty-eighth Street to buy drumsticks, and it felt so normal, a girl and a guy out, friends, doing a simple chore. I liked all the neatly arranged rows of musical instruments and the amiable salesman. I ambled about the big store, thought being a musician must be the best way to make a living, and wondered if anyone thought I was Marc's girlfriend. I wondered about that, too, and it remained a conversation we never had.

On an early Sunday evening, Marc, Joey, Sting, and I were the only people at CBGB, and that was pretty nifty. The place was closed and dark. I half hid behind Marc and Joey and smiled to myself as I thought about this newsworthy meeting. Sting was the front man for The Police, so he wasn't yet so famous, but he was well on his way. A brief encounter occurred with a pleasant Sting. "Hello. Nice to meet you. Have a good night." Sting was just okay-looking, but Marc quickly ushered me out of there. Meeting Sting was a coup. I could barely wait to tell Jill, but I had to wait until I got home, and when I did, we collapsed in mirth.

"Well, what was he like?" she asked.

"He was okay and nice. He said hi."

At the Mudd Club, a great place for a while located at 77 White Street in deserted lower Manhattan—lovely Mary Wells, for a brief, shiny moment Motown's biggest star ("My Guy" sold millions) performed in a blue sparkly gown—Marc drank away his paycheck, bottle after green bottle of beer. I loved the performance and loved being out on a big date, but after the show, I sat and waited and sat, hour after hour, as the place emptied out. That was not fun, and the drinking frightened me. I didn't know what to do; eventually, just about everyone left, and the lights came on. It was a long night that lasted until the break of day. For me to stay out all night, my parents must have been away on vacation. Otherwise, I wouldn't have been there. His drinking was a big part of our dates. I was too naïve to recognize an alcoholic, but I did know something was way wrong and was relieved to finally leave in the early morning with the bright sun shining on the still-closed lofts and warehouses of downtown. We emerged: I in my evening-out clothes, Marc in a stupor. I helped him into a cab and felt tired but still pleased to be with him.

He wore dark glasses.

"Put your sunglasses on," he said.

I did, and then he kissed me. Finally.

The Mudd Club turned out to be a bittersweet place where I had my cherished camera stolen. It was dark and so packed you had to be on your guard, but that didn't deter us. Jill, Daniel, and I went often. Our friend Richard Smith worked there, so not only did he let us in, but we didn't pay either. The other hopefuls who awaited entrance looked at us longingly, in secret, as we, the downtown celebrities, slipped through the line. The club showcased a scene with all kinds of provocative people. Elderly-looking, avant-garde writer and opiate enthusiast William S. Burroughs participated as a frequent patron. (In the early 1940s, Burroughs had encouraged Jack Kerouac and Allen Ginsberg to write, and remained their close friend and teacher.)

"Come here." Richard Smith pulled us aside in his attempt to educate us, the dumbbells. "That is the author William S. Burroughs. He wrote *Naked Lunch* and put a glass on his wife's head and shot her dead through her forehead." Our teacher waited for our reactions.

"Why did he do that?" I asked. Why wasn't he in jail? I wondered.

"They were playing William Tell."

We all looked at the elderly gent. He was a little younger than the ghostly *clericus* who appears in *Drugstore Cowboy*.

Old Bull Lee, dressed in a gray suit, lounged with one leg crossed over the other, undisturbed. A faint smile adorned his face. Perhaps he pondered his bizarre life or desired a Viennese waltz, or maybe he sat in a haze of H, remembering days in Putumayo or Algiers or his house in the New Orleans swamp. Or maybe he quietly recited Shakespeare in his mad old mind. Jill and I noted his presence and giggled and gazed at him. Never in our wildest imagination would we have thought of saying hello, but I wished I had. I wished I'd spoken to the old rascal, and I wished I'd done that terribly unchic, un-hip thing and asked him for an autograph, or had the nerve to take a photo with him! I could have sat on his bony knee and that would have been a funny, funny picture. But sophisticated me did none of those things.

Knowing that Burroughs was an author of note, I tried to capture his worn face in my memory and grew fond of him , from a distance, the way a child might like a scary figure in a horror movie. I probably won't read *Naked Lunch*, but years later I did read excerpts from *Junkie* and was impressed by his brilliant, clear prose. Recently hearing a taped recording of Burroughs's routines revealed a grouchy old man's voice, and he reminded me of a mean doctor from my childhood. That very stern, creepy doctor had had no patience and pushed me out of his office. I didn't know what Burroughs was talking about on the recording: Roosevelt and baboons with purple hindquarters—he hated bureaucracy and liberals—but I still found him most amusing. Burroughs proved his intelligence to me. How much better for him to dwell among the youth and vitality and live performance and pretty faces at the Mudd Club than to languish away at home or behind the doors of a senior facility. His drug administration must have been meticulously careful. He lived until the age of eighty-three. Perhaps one of the best insights into the colorful life of Burroughs is in *On the Road: The Original Scroll*:

"'Hurry up, please. It's time,'" called the bartender. We hurried. In the words of T.S. Eliot, "'Goonight, Bill.'"

With our light complexions, long dark hair and dark eyes, and slender frames, Marc and I could have passed for brother and sister, or at least members of the same club. Like a big brother, Marc gave me a white Ramones T-shirt with blue letters. Maybe that was meant as a sign of affection, and I beamed. But he needed a clean shirt and took it back with the promise to get me another. He didn't. That was the only gift he ever almost gave me. He told me to wear blue jeans. They never fit, and I seldom did. The waist was always too big. His friend with the unwashed feet wore unlaundered blue jeans with down-in-the-heels, high-heeled sandals. He admonished me for being too thin, and hurt my feelings. "You're too skinny. Gain some weight and get womanly." Thoroughly insulted, I shot him a look of poisoned daggers. I was what I was, still only ninety-six pounds.

However, Marc expressed an unexpected compliment: I had good timing, good rhythm, and could keep the beat. Coming from him, that was high praise. Maybe Jill and I should have had our own band. We could have called it The Lipsticks, rat-a-tat-tat.

I almost met Marc's mother once, but he didn't introduce us. "Stay in the cab," he said. I gingerly waved to her, said hi through the window, and felt bad. Why hadn't he introduced us? She had a concerned look on her face, as if to ask: Who is this girl? Who are her parents? Where does she come from, and what's she doing with my son? She was a perfectly respectable- looking mother who worked at Brooklyn College, and I was a skinny, young, demure girl wearing rather strange downtown clothes and trying to look street-smart, like the junkie girl with dirty feet.

The closest Marc came to meeting my parents was when he met Kris, my oldest sister. She had driven Jill and me to a concert and escorted us backstage. He was polite and friendly to her, and always nice to Jill. With good reason, my parents didn't like any of the boys we liked, so there was no reason or cause to present Marc.

Marc's twin brother Fred came around on occasion. Fred resembled a young Warren Beatty, but whenever he appeared at the clubs he was always falling-down inebriated and angry. He frightened me and asked me for money once. I said no. Rumor spread that he'd had a car accident on the Brooklyn Bridge. His girlfriend had been thrown through the windshield and been decapitated. I never knew if that story was true, but when I started writing this memoir Fred appeared to me in a nightmare as a ghoul.

The relationship with Marc lasted for about a year. During that time I traveled with the band twice, once to California and the other time on tour to Washington, D.C.; Baltimore and Ocean City, Maryland; Virginia Beach; and Raleigh, North Carolina. It was July 1979. Monte, the driver—who lived in Queens—had fellow Queens residents Dee Dee and his wife Vera in the van already. Marc and I were the second stop in Brooklyn; so far, so good. Everyone proved amiable. We picked up Joey and his girlfriend at the loft around the corner from CBGB. Joey was good, Girlfriend not so. The last stop was Johnny and his girlfriend on East Tenth Street. As the van filled up, so did tensions, and I wondered what I

was doing there. Without words, it was apparent not everyone liked each other. However, things in the van were organ-
ized, legal, and businesslike. It was, after all, a moneymaking
enterprise financed by moneymen. The van remained pretty
quiet most of the time. Dysphoric Girlfriend did the most
talking; I did the least. She flipped through *People* and provided a running commentary. "Look at this one! She's a cow!
Look at that hair!" Girlfriend seemed absorbed in celebrity
magazines.

We made the long drive from Flatbush to Washington,
D.C., or to whichever gig came first. There was a little time
before the concert, so we did some sightseeing from the van.
It was getting dark, and the capitol city lit up. That was fun,
seeing the white marble city with the band. Driving over the
wide expanse of the Chesapeake Bay Bridge-Tunnel, looking
out at the miles of water, I thought of death. Suppose we go
over the side? Suppose we go in the tunnel and don't come
out? Suppose I never get home again? Monte was a good
driver. It was a new, safe van, and nothing happened.

Baltimore, Ocean City, and Virginia Beach passed by. I
can't recall stopping to eat a single meal or eating anything at
all. Of course, we had to eat, but I remember little about that
trip other than the concerts being great and loving the music.

Somewhere in those parts, some kid asked little me for an
autograph. Wow. How crazy! Marc didn't like that and
scowled at me as if I was trespassing into a place I didn't belong,
but I didn't mind, quickly scribbled down my name, and smiled
at the boy, because I was being nice to my one and only fan.

Gazing out at miles of tobacco leaves, we arrived in the beautiful city of Raleigh on a warm sunny afternoon. I felt sad and alone. Marc was subdued and under pressure—the new kid on the block—and I felt shy with this group of strangers who happened to be a rock legend in the making.

Hardcore, spiky-haired, cheek-pierced punk kids showed up at the concerts, and the band seemed repulsed and apprehensive about them. They feared physical harm. Many of those kids seemed lost and in search of something, a place to belong, and their appearance was disconcerting. The sound at the shows pulsed at an unbelievably loud level. My brain rattled, my ears shook, and my body rolled. Standing next to the speakers, having my hearing destroyed, I listened to the band play fast and furiously, and they were great at what they did. They were a unique band, an American original. It was big fun. I stood on the side, watched Marc, and looked out at the audience, mostly young males, very few girls. After the concert, an exhausted Marc dripped with sweat, his hair plastered to his head, his wet clothes clinging to his skin. The others were equally drenched and drained, like athletes after a game, a fighter after a match. It was hard work for them and fun for me to have had the adventure, but I was happy when the van dropped me off in Brooklyn, and I returned home to tell Jill my tales.

Marc asked me to go on a tour somewhere in the Midwest, but common sense prevailed and I said no. I had to work. I never knew when the phone would ring and Marc would ask me to go someplace. It was usually spur of the moment. He traveled almost constantly, and I didn't know when I would see him. My feelings about the trips and the relationship were a carnival ride of anxiety and delight. I was a girl pulling petals from a rose. Will he call? Won't he call? Will he call? Won't he? I was in limbo, anxious, and didn't like it. I was on pins and needles, needles and pins, needles and pins. My role remained undefined, and I had to explain my actions and whereabouts to my parents. I mumbled some fabricated nonsense to them to make the trips seem like a business arrangement, a job in the making. I'm sure they saw right through my shallow duplicity, but they let it go. Hardest of all was explaining myself to myself. I didn't know what I was doing. Still, who'd want to pass up who knows what? and I hoped for the best.

Before the tour, I traveled to Los Angeles for about three weeks in May 1979. Phil Spector was producing the album *End of the Century*, and that was a big thing. He had a long career and had worked with the band of all bands, The Beatles. Joey had a true rock 'n' roll voice: "Rock, rock, rock, rock, rock 'n' roll high school..." He leaned into the mike with his tall body and pushed his long curly hair out of his eyes the way he did on stage. He'd sing and then cut, sing and cut, over and over again. His sweet voice and the song sounded great, and I hoped to hear it just once without interruption, but I wasn't the maestro Phil—the Oz behind the curtain, the boy genius from the Bronx, the wizened wizard of record producing at the control board. Joey got hot and tired—the

leather jacket came off, and his face glistened—and I didn't
stay there until the end, hours and hours, take after take later.
Monte took me back to my room. Still, I thrilled to have been
there, listening to Joey and watching the recording process at
Gold Star studios. What kid wouldn't have loved it?

Visiting Capitol Records on a sunny afternoon as something of a minor VIP with the band was exciting, too. The
whole group packed into the van, and off we drove. The office workers in their corporate clothes were friendly, and I in
my black spandex and Ian's pumps was happy not to be one
of them. We were given a tour and met someone in a big office. It didn't last long, but it was fun to be one of the cool
kids, the coolest of the cool, and the whole group was happy.
Vintage black-and-white footage shows The Beatles at the
same circular, landmark Capitol Records building on Vine
Street in Hollywood.

In the evening, Phil invited us all to his rambling mansion
in the California hills. Wow. Won't that be fun? An electric
gate surrounded the Mediterranean villa. The inside was spacious and nondescript. He possessed a jukebox with just his
hits. A framed autograph photo of John and Yoko casually
on display impressed me. Talk circulated among the band
about Spector and his famously eccentric, paranoid ways, but
they seemed keen and honored to work with him. Maybe this
would be their big break, out of CBGB and onto the world
stage. Phil proved disagreeable and seemed to enjoy other
people's unease. Needless to say, I hid in back of Marc for as

long as I could. As the evening progressed, Phil asked everyone in the group what type of pizza to order, and it turned
into a big Spector production. When it came my turn, I said,
"Plain is fine," and "Mr. Wall of Sound" imitated my sound,
which happened to be my very soft, very distinct voice, in
front of the group. No one laughed, not even Girlfriend, and
I was very grateful. However, I wished I had never come and
wanted the floor to open up and swallow me. It didn't, so I
endured a long, long evening with Phil. For a while, I occupied a couch with the actor Al Lewis, Grandpa from the television program *The Munsters*. Politely drunk, he said hello.
He looked at me, I looked at him, and that was about it for
conversation.

All night at Phil Spector's house, with the view of Los Angeles's twinkling lights below, the time dragged and seemed
forever and was a bore. It was more fun to say I was there
than to actually be there. It would be a story to tell Jill. The
Ramones humored Phil along—their career was at stake—but
their good humor was short lived. Phil turned out to be impossible, and that's been well documented in other accounts
amid claims of wild exaggerations and accusations: something
about Dee Dee and Phil, and a gun in the recording studio.
Numerous tales of this incident exist, and all eliminate one
person: me. I had had more than my fill of Phil and turned
off the talk about him in my head. Perhaps as a blessing in
disguise, a lot of bad Taco Bell-type Mexican food sent me to
the emergency room, and I traveled home on the red-eye from
California alone, not disappointed to leave but going with the

feeling someone else was coming in my place, maybe the one with the dirty feet or the tall one.

Throughout those trips, I was an observer—now, I wished I had kept a journal—though little really happened, just a lot of bickering and banal talk to break up the long stretches on the road. The couples didn't socialize. This one hated that one; this one wasn't speaking to the other, so much friction. Sometimes there would be breaks of laughter, usually between Marc and Dee Dee, and sometimes Joey, but almost always the air was tense, so tense that I could have used my little white-handled knife to cut it, but I had prudently thrown it far, far away.

Mr. Joey Ramone loved rock 'n' roll. He was one of those passionate devotees who seemed to know every song ever recorded. In the van, he talked about Leslie Gore; everything you wanted to know about Leslie, he knew. The New Jersey girl was best known for her hit single at age sixteen, "It's My Party." He seemed enthralled by popular culture and watched a lot of television and movies.

Jeff—really more Jeffrey than Joey—was in poor health. Girlfriend frequently dispensed him medication. Johnny kept to himself and rarely seemed happy, and the impish Dee Dee was usually in a good mood but had a knack for getting in trouble even under the watchful eye of his kindly wife, Vera. His reckless binges left her crying.

Joey's then-girlfriend was mean and had the demeanor of a pit bull guard dog. She loved disco and Studio 54. Her favorite word was the "n" word, followed by the "f" word. Sometimes, she strung the two words together—quite a nasty piece, that girl. Oops! "You might very well think that," Frances Urquhart; "I couldn't possibly comment." She could ignore and scorn me; I didn't care. Girlfriend had plenty of smiles for everyone else, for me only acid looks of contempt. Fine, nothing about her was of consequence, but I wanted to lash out. In my head, I did: "Shut up, you idiot!" In an already electric atmosphere, I could have made a scene and given the whole gang something to remember me by. But the whole mostly tense experience of being with this group of semi-strangers, far from home, was too intimidating. I was too young and too docile to know how to handle it. I was little and small, a stranger in a strange place, and not feeling smart. It didn't help that I was a natural beauty, and pit bull girl hated that. I could easily imagine the little beast grabbing onto my ankle with her pointy, razor-sharp teeth. Girlfriend was absolutely furious when I innocently—stupidly but without malice—took three photographs, to show Jill, of course, of her and Joey in bed. They stayed there all day watching junk television. They were fully clothed and all—she wore red spandex—nothing going on, they just stayed in the sofa bed all day. Marc and I had come into their room to talk to Joey. I had my trusty camera in hand and just did what came naturally: *paparazzi, paparazzo, paparazza,* mosquito.

Ironically, before meeting Marc, Jill and I had met Joey once in front of CBGB. He'd been alone. We had asked him to take pictures with us, and he'd happily complied. There's a photo of Jill with a smiling Joey, and one of me with Joey. We look pretty good together. It would make a great book cover. Girlfriend was thwarted before we even met by me, the roving photographer. It's hard to conjure that she really liked Joey, but he had a foot in the hall-of-fame door for her, not that she seemed to know or like rock 'n' roll. Pre-girlfriend, we even managed to visit the loft at East Second Street that Joey shared with the rather standoffish Arturo, the Ramones' artistic director. There wasn't much furniture, but racks of silk-screened T-shirts with the Ramones' eagle filled the space.

I have a photo of Vera and Girlfriend seated on an ugly, brown-striped hotel couch, gazing at a magazine. They easily engaged in chatter, until I came along with my ubiquitous camera. Girlfriend looks directly at the photographer, me, with a most unpleasant expression. Vera wears a leopard-skin dress. Girlfriend wears green spandex with black tights; her skin and hair are white as milk, and her hand is clasped against her chest in protest revealing fingers with short blood-red enameled nails. She looks like Caligula in the 1977 series *I, Claudius*, but is not as sweet. The gals both have platinum hair and wear so much makeup they've given their faces new faces. Girlfriend flipped the pages of the magazine saying, "Here's a pretty nigga. There's a pretty nig. . . ." Unbelievable. She spent a lot of time discussing her rich ex-boyfriend and her father, who supported her and sent her money so she could go shopping. She didn't work. Wow, I thought. She can do whatever she wants, no parental interference at all, no restrictions, no clauses. She can live with her rock 'n' roll boyfriend in his loft right on the Bowery and travel around with nary a word of disapproval, and she gets money for shopping!

Vera, who was always a lady, never mean, treated me kindly and made the California trip better. She also provided some unsolicited financial advice. "Don't let Marc know how much money you have." I was a little taken aback. I didn't have much, but I was willing to listen to her, the matriarch. "I don't let Dee Dee know how much money I have," she said. Vera gently advised that Marc wasn't a good choice for me. She knew Marc better than I did and spent a lot of time traveling with him, so she knew his two strange women friends, too. I didn't want to seem a fool, so I told Vera that Lenny Kaye seemed interested and sent me postcards from Europe signed with *xxx* and *love*.

"He's a nice guy," she said, nodding. "He'd be better."

She told Girlfriend. "Yeah," she said, bored. "He'd be betta."

Nothing ever developed with Lenny, just postcards from across the ocean.

Vera was correct about Marc but would have done well to look at her own precarious situation.

The expensively scented, alabaster-skinned, manicured, painstakingly coiffed, immaculately groomed Vera seemed at mismatched opposites with the ripped-jeans, wanton Dee Dee, and that observation regards outward appearances only. The gold-hooped earrings and glitzy glamour of Vera was way out of place at the cave-like, bare-boned cavity that was CBGB, or any other downtown or shabby club we visited. Vera had no pretensions of being an artist or cutting-edge rock 'n' roller or bohemian. She was solidly middle class with middle-class values and a stable middle-class job, and would have been better suited to borough discos and polished disco men. No rough edges appeared on Vera. She was as smooth as the silk scarf tied at her throat. Dee Dee was as rough-and-tumble as the peeling, flyer- plastered walls or concrete pavement of 315 Bowery. Emotionally, she was the mature, patient parent; he was the rebellious son. If I hadn't been so polite, I would have asked how in the world those two, not only met, but married.

I never had a real conversation with Joey. His girlfriend, the guard, of course, wouldn't allow it, and I shied away. Even while sitting in bed with her, he always wore dark glasses, so his eyes weren't visible. He was tall, with a terribly slouched posture and an uneasiness around me that was probably due to Girlfriend.

Marc broke things up with his antic disposition. He seldom, if ever, called me by my name. Sometimes I wondered if he knew it. He called me baby (pronounced baay-*bee*) in this loud, maniacal way. "Hi, bay-*bee*!" which caused people to look. Calling on the phone, he did the same. In that boisterous voice, Marc called Dee Dee "Brucie": "Hiya, Bruc-*ee!*" he shouted, and fluttered his eyes and waved his hands and looked and sounded like Milton Berle. Dee Dee certainly laughed. Marc was amused. It was funny, rip-roaringly hysterical. Girlfriend didn't find it funny and focused on me with yet another look of ill-tempered contempt.

Since elementary school, I'd always had a soft spot for the class clown, and Marc certainly fit the bill. At the Motel Tropicana in California, he had no swim attire, so he sat outside in his black underpants. He colored his hair and went outdoors to lounge in the sun with black dye dripping down his head. I took pictures of that memorable scene. It was Marc's way of going Hollywood. He was always extremely entertaining, and I was always a stellar audience. Years later, still hurt but thinking myself all grown up, I tossed those photos. All that remains is one picture of Vera and Girlfriend, and an official autographed photo of all four Ramones dressed in their black-leather Schott jackets, ripped jeans, and sneakers. Marc's the best looking and has the best posture. He's next to Johnny and standing apart from the others. After throwing away the pictures, I gave away all the albums to a sad lost boy who liked their records and had a sad lost band of his own.

Marc had an exaggerated comic presence with all kinds of funny faces and funny voices. He had an outburst over the phone with his landlord and kept yelling about a problem with the refrigerator. "I won't pay the rent," he threatened. It wasn't what he said but how he said it, in a deep, low, teeth clenched, controlled voice, that struck me as gut-wrenchingly funny. I bit my lip and ran into another room to bury my face in a cushion to muffle the sounds of my yawp. I didn't want him to hear me. But another problem arose with that same refrigerator that was not funny at all and troubled me. On top of it was a stack of foreign porn magazines. I knocked against something, and they all came crashing to the floor. I didn't see much—half-naked tootsies wearing little maids' aprons—but I was embarrassed and offended, though I didn't say anything. Wasn't porn for pathetic, lonely, dirty old men? Why would a young guy have that? It felt wrong.

In Los Angeles, simmering tensions turned into a full rolling boil. Marc had an absolute tantrum about an argument with the band regarding T-shirt money. The shirts sold at concerts, and because Marc wasn't an original member, he wasn't getting a cut. I don't know what happened first—a phone call to his father the longshoreman lawyer, or what I vaguely remember as him destroying the television? He kept saying over and over "Dad.... Dad.... Dad...." and again, I had to find a way to control my bouts of laughter, the kind that hurts, and tears come spilling down your face, and you're afraid of bursting your side.

His outrage was not for me to handle, and someone, probably calm, reasonable Monte, the reliable, sane, patient road manager, had to come and stop it. "Hey, hey, hey! What the hell's going on? Calm down. Cut it out! Get a grip. What the hell happened to the television? What's the *matter* with you? You can't *do* that."

Had Marc been drunk before Monte came or after? Monte was quiet, serious, and had sad, puppy-dog eyes. He seemed older than the others and liked me. I was comfortable with Monte. I liked him as a friend and was grateful to him for his kindness and good sense. We talked to each other. Like a wise sage with kind, rabbinical eyes, he advised me against Marc, too. "You're a nice girl," he said. "Marc can sometimes get out of control." Marc's drinking could get way out of hand, and I didn't see the worst of it because I usually was with him when he was on the job and couldn't overindulge.

When we were in Hollywood, Monte and Marc took me to Frederick's of Hollywood, where I bought a pair of high-heeled silver mules and wore them until they fell apart. The leather was soft, and when the shoes broke, I discovered the heel was constructed with a metal spike. On the same shopping spree, I also bought a purple-and-black lace bustier. I had nothing to corset, so, much to my disappointment, I couldn't wear the thing. Later, with the other girls, including Girlfriend, we went to Fiorucci's, where I bought the beloved black spandex pants. I was so happy that something finally fit, I wore those pants until they frayed at the seams. Wanting to keep up with the well-painted other girls, I wore blue eye shadow and red lipstick, hoping to look like an Andy Warhol painting, but I probably just looked silly.

The band stayed at the infamous Tropicana Motel on Santa Monica Boulevard in West Hollywood, where old Los Angeles died and a host of others, including Jim Morrison, had at one time lived. My parents would have shunned that place and thought it tawdry. It wasn't that bad, really. It was clean and tidy. When I announced my trip to California, my mother had reacted, "Why in the world do you want to get involved with a rock band?"

I'd replied, "Because I have the chance." Poor Mom—I wish I hadn't done that to her. What mother would want her daughter to travel with the Ramones?

The British girl-pretty Levi and the Rockats were at the Tropicana, too, displaying mass body tattoos—which I found repulsive—on their thin, milky-white bodies at the hideous black swimming pool. Personality Chuck E. Weiss ("Chuck E's in Love"), a friend of Tom Waits, hung there, too. What exactly he did, I don't know, but he was there. A picture of a black- bikinied Chuck was tossed with the photos of Marc. I had photos of Marc, Dee Dee, and me at the pool, too, sitting around. That was when Dee Dee had a single heart tattoo on his arm. We were all laughing. I was wearing a big smile and little black dress, and my long black hair was cut in bangs. For a short time, I was proud of those bangs. It was Johnny's sweet wife who'd cut them for me, so I wore the bangs as a sign of secret acceptance and with my leather jacket: *I was a Ramone, too.* My happiness deflated when Marc said I looked like Cher. He meant it as a compliment, but I didn't want to look like Cher, whom I thought was a thoroughly silly creature.

There was a noisy, always crowded New York-style deli next to the Tropicana where we ate often with Monte, sometimes with Dee Dee, but never with the others, who seldom seemed to leave their rooms. In those young and very skinny days, food wasn't important.

Besides for the outburst and the pool, my other memory of the Tropicana was agreeing to cook Marc a healthy dinner. He was in self-imposed exile for a few days after the T-shirt debacle, and I was expected to be part of the lockdown. I didn't know how to cook but decided to make fish and broccoli with garlic and olive oil. Marc liked it. The suite became smoky and smelled of fried cloves. I was totally embarrassed, opened all the windows, and hoped Girlfriend wouldn't notice. After the olive oil and garlic haze, Marc started to call me in that loud funny voice his sexy Italian. "Hiya, sexy Italian bay-*bee*." I stood there mirthfully yowling my head off. Of course, it was hilarious, and naturally, it gave Girlfriend another chance to scowl. When I asked Marc about his ethnicity, he said he was Presbyterian. I didn't believe him. He didn't look Presbyterian. The Presbyterians I knew were nice little white-haired ladies. I smiled many years later, after reading, in the *Heebie-Jeebies at CBGB: A Secret History of Jewish Punk*, the author, Steven Lee Beeber, describes Marc as being Italian.

Johnny said he could survive all year on a couple of hundred dollars by eating tuna every day, buying one pair of jeans, and a pair of sneakers. All his T-shirts came free from promotions, practical fellow. None of the Ramones was handsome, but John had beautiful shiny hair. He was intimidating; his reserve didn't allow for many smiles. I don't think he ever even looked at me, and if he had, I would have trembled. His pretty, Jewish, Middle Eastern-born first wife was more engaging than his present girlfriend, though I thought the girlfriend might just have been shy, too. He kept her on a short leash. Rumor had it, he beat her. A neighbor who lived in their East Tenth Street building told of the beatings and screams, and of seeing her swollen and black-and-blue. Later, books and riches in patience and kindness.

My husband is a musician, too. He almost made it to the stage of CBGB. A group of musical friends and he had the original idea of switching instruments with each other and playing what they didn't know how to play—as a parody of the entire downtown "too cool to be true" scene—but at the last minute a Yalie named Malcolm withdrew, because he was afraid of appearing un-hip, and the event didn't happen. The world never saw the Montclair Four.

But the world—a very small portion of the world, minus William F. Buckley—did see Mal perform, well, accompany one Allen Ginsberg on a hip but sad New Haven stage in that beaten sirens screeching into the gloomy New England night of an urban downtown. The bearded, bespectacled bard provided a poetry reading, and Mal was chosen to stand behind him and strum his guitar. The coolly intellectual Malcolm was about as nervous as a wallflower on the night of the senior prom. "What am I going to wear? What will I say to him?" and Mal worked himself up poring over the epic William Carlos Williams poem *Paterson* and relating it to Ginsberg's own experience of growing up there, near the Great Falls in the Old Silk City. Malcolm had his moment. He stuttered and spewed and finally got out a whole lot of nonsense.

"Well, I do believe William Carlos Williams, and for that matter Walt Whitman, oh, yes, and Blake, Blake, too, were trying to say. . . ." and on and on he rambled like a date who is trying way too hard to make a good first impression.

The amorous Ginsberg gently draped his arm around

it proved not to be a rumor but true and documented in other books. The poor woman seemed isolated and under his thumb. There were several rumors about her. One was that she was part of old-money New York aristocracy. Her bad teeth made that hard to believe. The other claimed she was a "dancer." That was easier to believe, because she looked the part with her curvy figure, early Cynthia Lennon long blonde processed hair, light lipstick, and dark glasses. No matter what or who she was, I felt badly for her; though we never spoke, she was pleasant and from time to time wore a faint smile. I should have pulled her aside and said: Run! Get out of there. That's a bad place to be, even if it means giving up your nice East Tenth Street apartment and your boyfriend with the beautiful hair and rock band. Run, run, run away! But, I didn't.

My role with Marc and the Ramones was often confused, tense, and uncomfortable. If older and more mature, I would have realized that the deep, long-time animosity in those relationships had nothing to do with me. But being a self-conscious young thing, I felt maybe it did. They had serious conflicts with each other and with themselves. It was far from an ideal situation to be there.

Dee Dee was the most approachable, but we didn't talk either. We just said hi, smiled, laughed, and then Marc would break in with his clowning, and they'd be off. And that was just fine with me. Dee Dee's dark side was well known to others, but he was always joking and fun to me.

There was one cute guy with the Ramones. He was a

roadie, Joey the Roadie, and he was called "Joey the Roadie" so as not to be confused with Joey the Ramone. There was a hierarchy, and poor wannabe rock star Joey the Roadie was treated as, well, a roadie and not very kindly—except by Marc, because Joey the Road was his friend from Brooklyn. Joey the Roadie kind of looked like Harry the kid in *Requiem for a Dream*. I was afraid to befriend sad, sweet Joey the Road because I knew he'd start to like me if I was nice to him, so I had to keep my distance.

The comedy of many errors came to its finale. The last time I saw the Ramones was behind the scenes at a concert in Central Park on August 6, 1979. Backstage was a small world of girlfriends; an ex-wife; Sylvain Sylvain, the tall, thin redhead; and the unsavory one with the dirty sandaled feet. One snarled at me, and then the other. Sharing the same hot space with those two lurching, feline creatures was unpalatable, out of the question. What else were we sharing? I didn't like any of it. It felt wrong and affronted my tender young dignity. This wasn't what I wanted. I had had enough and felt duped. There were just too many people back there to avoid, and no place to hide—the two creatures and Girlfriend looked for all the world like Macbeth's three witches. I wanted to scream at Marc, "Do you think I'm an idiot? Do you think I'm a fool? What's up with those two creatures?" There I was, a poor player, strutting and fretting upon the backstage, telling a tale, I the idiot, The Fool without cap and bells, full of sound and fury. I looked like Cordelia, then a mad Ophelia, but inwardly I raved like Lear.

I wrung my hands and wanted to wring his neck. All the frustrations and tensions and disappointments and anxieties and slights finally came to a head. Incensed, but trying to remain poised, I said my cool, hurtful good-bye to Marc: "You're a cad and a coward," words derived from romance stories. They sounded so antiquated, I might as well have said them in Latin. I was sad, because I liked him. He didn't say anything, but he appeared wistful, too.

Saying those words was easy because I was so, so angry with Marc. I could have said more, much, much more. I could have screamed with all my might. I could have started screaming, at the beginning of high school, at the fight in the cafeteria, at the cruel sewing teacher, at my friend the competitor, at my uncle's murderers, at the Cooper Union. I could have killed Mills, the dangerous predator, and screamed at my own stupidity, and screamed at Syl and at Phil Spector, and at not having enough money, and at not knowing what to do with my life. I could have screamed one big, horrible, primal scream to fill all of Central Park and wake up the zoo animals in their city cages, and all that noise could have added to the fray. Roar, mighty Aslan, roar! I could have smashed the drums and ripped the stage apart. I could have thrashed the creatures with my high heels, and throttled Girlfriend, and washed her mouth out with soap until she begged for mercy at the top of her voice, crying out in her stupid Long Island or whatever accent. I could have slashed everyone's leather jackets and just gone completely nuts, but I did none of those things because my mother had always cautioned that I should act like a lady. I didn't feel like a lady. I felt like a crazy punk rock kid who was enraged, but the last thing I wanted was to appear a fool, especially in front of the formidable Johnny Ramone. So I listened to my mother's advice, and she was right. It's always best to act like a lady. It was the giving up that was hard. You see, I truly liked Marc, really, I was deeply in love, but I never told him or anyone else, not even Jill, because I knew it was futile. He was the most fun, funniest person I ever met. I loved being with him and simply adored him, as all his friends adored him. And I had bright dreams for a future together.

I used to talk about Marc to a beatnik lady I knew from the public library. She was a hip old thing who wore her gorgeous white hair piled on top of her head in a big knot. She wore beautiful clothes and was quite educated. She rode on the train back and forth from New York, always alone. Apparently, her family was well to do, and she didn't work. Her brother had been the president of a bank, but he was serving a prison sentence for embezzling a lot of money. She was all alone except for her books and newspapers.

"No. *No!* Don't you understand?" she asked, looking into my eyes. "He's with someone different every night! He's on the road. He's a musician. You can't be with him." I didn't want to believe her, and in a way I think the two creatures kind of kept him reigned in, but I looked into the old woman's beautiful eyes and at her velvet skin, and, once again, I didn't want to be a fool in her view, either. My heart was a fool's heart. My mind was a young girl's mind, full of hopes of love and romance, but image was so important that I bit my lip and walked away from what I so intently longed for. I was a fool, but I wasn't going to let the whole world know it.

Looking back at that backstage scene, I should have said nothing and accepted what was and withdrawn without a whisper, accepting my unfulfilled hopes, our combined youth and inexperience. I don't recall many of our conversations. Maybe we had so few. Maybe the laughter sufficed. My time with the Ramones ended. I started to change and no longer enjoyed going out after midnight to clubs. I had graduated and didn't go to CBGB or Max's anymore. After a while, I threw away the spandex and stilettos from Ian's and started shopping at Brooks Brothers. I had a responsible job uptown. I never saw Marc, Dee Dee, or Joey again. But one summer day, on my way to work by the Astor Place subway station near Cooper Union, dressed in a soft silk dress, a navy blazer and Charles Jourdan pumps, I saw Johnny. He saw me, stopped, and smiled in approval, as if to say, *You did the right thing.*

I didn't read Legs McNeil and Gillian McCain's book *Please Kill Me: The Uncensored Oral History of Punk* until twenty-seven years after I last saw the Ramones. I learned more than I knew then. Few were portrayed in a flattering light or made to look even slightly attractive. All appear pretty deranged. I asked myself, Who were these people? The more important question being, What was I doing there? I hadn't known their histories, and much of what I read dis-

turbed me. I may have been in their company briefly, but I
hadn't known the personalities the very astute Legs revealed.
But he was a firmly entrenched member of that community,
and I'd just been floating by. Though we traveled in a van together, we, the band and I, never sat down to eat as a group.
That would have been a sign of friendship. Too quiet, too shy
to talk, I should have been asking questions. I silently watched
and then went home. *Please Kill Me* has a harsh voice; though
Marc sounds like Marc, his role is minimal. He was such a
funny and talented guy, his role should have been bigger.

Monte Melnick's *On the Road with the Ramones* provides an easier narrative than some of the other books. Then
again, Monte was a gentleman. As a group, we did all pile
into the van with virtuous Monte—the driver and babysit-
ter—and go to an LA club, either the Whisky A-Go-Go or The
Roxy, to see a sensational Robert Gordon. Everyone was
happy that night and had a good time. It was like going on a
class trip, a class trip with the Ramones, and that was fun,
great fun—*On the Road*, indeed.

I saw the excellent documentary *End of the Century* for
the first time in March 2009. Remarkably, no one had
changed much at all from those early days. They retained
their boroughness and borough accents, which I found funny.
End of the Century is a mirror reflection of all.

About ten years after I had left the Ramones far in my past
and graduated from college, I was setting out to make a new
life: no more Millses, Marcs, or Andrews. I wanted a stable,

secure relationship and was dating a criminal lawyer I referred to in my head as "Hey Uptight Old Mr. Normal." I mentioned living in the East Village and showed him some photographs. He said I looked like the Robert Palmer girls with my dark hair tied back and black clothes. (I had done that look first.) Well, I never heard the end of it from him, who called me an East Village "weirdo." He used the East Village to mock me, and because of that, I wanted to erase that part of my history. His hostile teasing was the extent of the dullard's creativity. That's when I tossed the funny pictures of Marc with the hair dye and Joey and Girlfriend in red spandex, unique photos of rock 'n' roll history gone forever, photographs that could have made people laugh. That's an example of how one person can change the world. I was usually generous with my photos, so who knows? Maybe I made copies for Marc that he kept.

After an evening with the up-and-coming, high-income law firm partner, which felt like an exhausting night of babysitting for a really trying adolescent, I was wiped out. The relationship ended abruptly by phone. He cancelled a date for the upcoming holiday weekend. Months later, he got married, so he was dating his soon-to-be bride and me at the same time. Ironically, his schizophrenic brother, Len, was fond of me. Len and I remained friends for twenty years, and from that friendship I established another extraordinary friendship and a lasting and happy marriage to an exquisitely aristocratic, gently mannered, handsome, and beloved husband who is in a refined class of his own—and rich as a impecunious Lampedusa, with as many books as Lampedusa: a fortune in

Malcom, asked, "Do you know any Hank Williams songs?" and led him away.

At the same time as "Hey Uptight," a young doctor of internal medicine showed up. They were each other's counterpart: professional, mean-spirited, adolescent types. After a few expensive, tense dinners, I had a strong feeling Dr. Strangelove was a Mills. After he aggressively demanded a ride from the airport, I let him have it and blew up. "You idiot! In a long line of jerks, you're the biggest jerk I've ever met!" That was the end of that. I had the quaint notion that, once I had left the rough-and-tumble environs of post-industrial Perth Amboy, once I had left the Bowery, people, men, educated men, would behave as gentleman. Ha-ha, wrong again. Innocently, I thought the world would be a better place than it turned out to be.

"Hey Uptight" and Strangelove called to mind yet another incident floating in the recesses of my mind. At age thirteen, I met Jonathan, a boy who lived four or five blocks away. He was friends with a slightly older boy who lived across the street from me. Jonathan went to a Catholic boys' prep school in another town. His father was a bank president, his brother a priest, and his sister a school principal. Well, Jonathan, my neighbor, and I hung around for a while until it was time to go home. A few days later, Jonathan and I talked again on a nearby playground.

He asked me, "Do you know about oral sex?"

"No," I said. "And, I don't want to know." I had the sense

to run home. How smart I was at thirteen. I should have had the same sense to immediately run from all of them: Mills, Marc, Andrew, Uptight, and Strangelove. I shouldn't have acted big. I should have acted little to protect my tender innocence from the predatory Mills and those who followed. *To thine own self be true.*

Years after the playground, on the New Jersey Transit bus leaving Port Authority going back to Perth Amboy, Jonathan was on the bus and had the audacity to approach me. "Don't I know you?" he asked from his seat.

"No. You don't know me." I replied and kept moving.

Recently, when I was substitute-teaching at an affluent, suburban middle school, a boy was wearing a Ramones T-shirt. Wow, aren't there any new bands? I wanted to approach the kid and ask, Why are you wearing that? Why don't you have your own bands from your own generation? Why not make your own band? Why would a sixth-grader, twenty-five-plus years later, be interested? In Ridgewood, New Jersey, an upper-income Bergen County town, walking down the street was another boy wearing a Ramones T-shirt. All over, kids wear Ramones T-shirts.

Once in a while, a Ramones song is on a TV commercial. The other night on TV, a movie actor wore a Ramones T-shirt. I was surprised. In the public library, a book exists on the final resting places of rock stars. Three of the four Ramones I had traveled with died. Referring to the Ramones as rock stars was a revelation. Mick Jagger and Jim Morrison are rock stars, but Johnny, Dee Dee, Joey, and Marc Bell? Really? Lately, Ramones T-shirts have been on celebrities and ads all over the place. The last was Paris Hilton, on the Internet, wearing a pink Ramones T-shirt. They would have loved that.

As for the Ramones' "curse," how juvenile. Curse? No, that's life. People get seriously ill. People die. For those who engage in risky behavior, the outcome may be less than positive. Shoot dope, it might kill you. Engage in nasty business, you might be dealt a fatal blow. Bad things happen. Far more good things happened to the Ramones than bad. How many bands from Queens are inducted into the Rock and Roll Hall of Fame? They enjoyed many years of critical acclaim, commercial success, a certain fame, and fortune. How many young bands can actually make a living by just being in a band? Let's put things into perspective: Not every band is going to sell as many albums as The Beatles. I don't think the Ramones or anyone connected to them has anything to whine about. They worked hard, and they were also lucky.

Very, very ironically, I didn't see the 1979 Roger Corman B-movie *Rock 'n' Roll High School* until June 2007. It was absolutely silly, and the poor Ramones look completely ill at ease, but the music was great, and Marc gets a line. Each revealed something of his personality: wild Dee Dee, angry Johnny, Marc nervous with his arm crossed, and Joey the heartthrob? At the end of the film, the kids blow up the school. The same night we watched the DVD, borrowed from our affluent suburb's public library, which is next to the Town

Hall (where the police station is located), which is next to the high school, all of which is paid for by affluent taxpayer dollars, the AP news reported that five high school kids had been arrested over a "prank" involving pyrotechnic devices found at the high school. The school was evacuated one day before the start of final exams. The explosives had been found by a student who noticed fuses hanging from a locker. Officials said the damage would have been devastating. Isn't that a strange coincidence?

Last night I had a dream; the dream was in the present. We were at a big party. Joey, Dee Dee, and Johnny were there. Joey was happy, talking to me and giggling. Dee Dee was charmingly outgoing and hospitable, bringing me food and drinks. We talked a lot. Vera was happy, smiling, her lovely self. In the crowd, Johnny's shiny beautiful hair stood out, but he was unavailable—out of reach. Gradually he moved closer. He looked at his feet; he looked at me, and smiled, and said something nice. I asked Dee Dee where Marc was, but he wasn't there, and I was so disappointed. I asked Dee Dee about Marc's sobriety and his lip curled upward in a smile. I found my heart—my young heart—aching, though my hair was gray, and I was the only person present altered by age. My dress was sophisticated black wool, and my heels were elegant—grown-up clothes. Sensing my disappointment at Marc's absence and to make me feel better, Dee Dee said Marc's mother had made the salmon dip. Joey quipped, "But she forgot to put the salmon in it." Everyone laughed. The boys were clad in their eternal leather jackets. They always wore the uniform: T-shirts, jeans, and those leather jackets. Richard Hell passed by with a blank look. Band member Richard Quine wore his heavy black-framed glasses, and the angelic Ivan Julian smiled and walked by.

Gradually I felt Marc's presence. I could smell his milky breath and warm skin. His hair was dripping and plastered to his face. He wore that slightly scolding expression and didn't speak. I felt the warmth and weight of the worn leather jacket. I smelled the warm leather and touched its softness. I saw the pale skin and the thin arms, and that dream was very, very real to me, and I woke up, but they stayed with me for the night into the early morning.

Joey came to me in yet another dream. He was dressed in his black leather jacket and was joyfully ecstatic, radiating beatific happiness in a way I had never seen him. We sat so close that I could smell his clean skin. He pushed the dark, glossy hair out of his eyes and reminisced about old times. He confirmed what I'd said about Marc, and we laughed and spoke of Girlfriend and laughed even harder. When I woke up, I could still feel his warmth and see that glorious smile. I mentioned the dream to Kris, as I related the frustrations of being rejected by exactly one hundred and fifty literary agents: four were kind, three disdainful; the others had sent form letters or nothing. The form letters are most insulting of all. My sister said something truly comforting; "I don't think Joey Ramone would take a break from his heavenly delights if he wasn't trying to tell you something." Joey, Jeffrey didn't give up; year after year he stuck to his goal. I blessed his pure soul and prayed for the others, John and Dee Dee, Douglas Glenn, really. I thought of Johnny Thunders, John Anthony Genzale— named the names of holy saints—and thought of skeletal old William Burroughs, and said a prayer for them, too, poor suffering souls. Was Burroughs spending his time in purgatory reading Dickens aloud to Evelyn Waugh's mad Mr. Todd in the Brazilian jungle? Did he show fear in a handful of dust? Does he roam the windowless bunker at 222 Bowery? In a state of contemplation, I even said a prayer for sorry shrunken Phil Spector and the poor dead actress. The last time going-to-prison Phil was on television, he certainly looked like he could use some help. Then, I prayed for a twenty-something-year-old, a friend's son, who is destroying his family with his journey into heroin.

I rushed to the post office to mail yet another query and book proposal, this time to famed poet Lawrence Ferlinghetti, publisher and founder of City Lights Bookstore. The post office was officially closed. I was two minutes late but ran into the exit door as someone was leaving. "We're closed!" the irate manager yelled.

"Please! I have to mail this!" I swept past him as the few patrons in line ignored the minor scene I had created and I handed my manila envelope to the disgruntled clerk and hoped he wouldn't toss it after I left. I felt a little like would-

be Andy Warhol assassin Valerie Solanas, who had taken infamous extremes but finally gotten published.

A few weeks later came yet another rejection letter, signed
by a City Lights assistant.

City Lights and friends had written the books on breaking the rules, and so I decided to do the same. I had been
scrupulously obedient about following publishers' and
agents' submission guidelines, but now it was my turn to
rebel. I made a copy of the entire unsolicited manuscript
and wrote a poem to the poet laureate of far-out, flipped,
wavy gravy San Francisco, named for the holy fool of Assisi.
I printed it on the best- quality bond paper and sent it out,
chagrined about having been labeled a kook, but figured
Larry could handle one more. Remarkably, a week later, another City Lights envelope came in the mail. I hesitated to
open it. In a handwritten letter on the bookstore's stationery, Mr. LF said he couldn't publish my manuscript but
thanked me for my poem. I was so wound up, I couldn't sit
still or sleep that night. A few days before, I had gleefully
sent him a revision of the poem in hopes that he liked it.
Now for sure, I would be thought at worst nuts, at best a
Ms. Nuisance.

> *Lawrence Ferlinghetti Spaghetti,*
> *What sauce do you toss?*
> *Unto the ages of ages,*
> *He art in heaven.*
> *Saucy boy, ponder that*

as you approach the beatific throne.
Four feet good, two feet bad.
How can a starving poet eat
homemade all natural premium quality fusilli
or farfalle,
penne, rigatoni, fettuccine, or linguini,
ditalini, cavatelli, orrechiette, vermicelli, or rigatoni,
from finest golden semolina?
Was Marconi a phony?
Holden?
How does the unemployed consumer sauce
such sublime macaroni?

Well, LFS didn't appear enthralled with the poem. Maybe he didn't understand it, or maybe he did. He didn't say, but surely, someday, it will all matter not as it, he, and I return to from whence we came.

Thus far, the highlight of my literary career has been a two-line letter of rejection on good stationery from Sterling Lord, Jack Kerouac's literary agent.

In honor of Horatio Hornblower, I christened myself *Indefatigable*. Like a crazed hobbit, little and steadfast, or kamikaze with the task of slaying the publishing dragon, I soldiered on. As in *La Passion de Jeanne d'Arc*, I wept at my smug judges, and, late at night, collapsed on bent knees, cried in the voice of the psalmist to the vast literary landscape laid to waste: Where art thou, my Ezra Pound? And, like Fitzcarraldo inching that boat up the mountain for the sake of art, I kept going.

> *Golden lads and girls all must,*
> *As chimney-sweepers, come to dust*
> *—Cymbeline*

6

CHER, MARIO O O O CUOMO, VINCENT, AND JACKIE O

❦

CHER WAS KINDER TO ME than I was to her. I was young, insecure, shy, and arrogant. The pop queen Madonna was emerging at that time and we, my friends and I, dismissed her as something for the masses, not for the select few, the downtown socialites. Madonna was scorned and scoffed at by the downtowners, but, as we all know, she had the last laugh. Cher and Madonna would be in the same class: super, megarich stars. James, of the marriage proposal and parsimonious mother, practiced in the same studio space as M, but that was long ago, and that's as close as our paths crossed—unless you consider a sleek, enormous, James Bond-type yacht named *Lady M* docked at the marina in Halifax, Nova Scotia. Word circulated it belonged to Madonna, and I felt proud of not contributing a farthing to that overflow. Apparently, she didn't need the patronage of the downtown set. In comparison, moored off Edgartown, in Martha's Vineyard, was the old, boxy *Blue Guitar*. In the world of yachts, it was without grace and looked like a tub. It had clearly seen better days. Word went around that it belonged to Eric Clapton. The bigger the yacht, the less visible the owner.

Why I found Clapton's yacht particularly astounding was this: To the rock 'n' roll savvy of my generation, Eric Clapton was the alpha and omega—he walked on water. His old boat was a huge disappointment not worthy of Mr. Slowhand. I suffered through one of his concerts once—he must have been going through a bad time and nodded out on stage, his fingers stuck on some tediously long solo. It was endless, and I doubled over in pain with severe monthly cramps in the hard arena seat, nauseated by the blanket of marijuana fumes that filled the Garden on a Saturday night, not wanting to distract my friends, who were transfixed by him.

Cher was in New York, working on Broadway in Robert Altman's play *Come Back to the 5 and Dime, Jimmy Dean, Jimmy Dean*. I was working as a makeup artist and skin care specialist at a well-known place on West Fifty-fifth Street. Eventually, Cher would be my client. At the time of hire, I knew so little about cosmetics that Jill applied my makeup for the interview. I sat still and, with Jill's expert hand and little jars and containers of cosmetics, she performed magic on me. I looked fantastically, clinically professional and wore a crisp, tailored fuchsia coatdress. Now, I had to demonstrate my skills on the owner's wife. The only problem was, I had no skills. I shook with apprehension and quickly appraised the *tabula rasa* sitting in front of me. Droopy eyelids needed to be righted, where there were none cheekbones needed to be created, and thin lips had to be filled out. I applied green eye shadow too far up and out, drew with a too bright lipstick on a pencil-straight lip, and painted cheeks with pink circles. Finished, she looked absurd, absolutely ridiculous—like an Andy Warhol silkscreen gone mad, a berserk Picasso with eyes going in different directions and lips askew, all painted with bright colors to give her pale skin some oomph. She smiled her thin smile at me and got up to show her husband. I had taken my art a little too far and wanted to die. If I hadn't been glued to my seat in complete dejection, I would have crept out the door, never, ever to return to the hard, merciless city that is New York. Incredibly, almost miraculously, I was hired anyway. The shop owner later told me he had been afraid I'd cry if I didn't get the job, and he didn't want to be the cause of those tears. He was that generous and unbelievably kind, but being so immature, I didn't fully appreciate him. I started my new job standing behind the shop counter, selling makeup I didn't know how to use.

Within the first few days, the owner took the staff to the cozy, old-fashioned Minetta Tavern for a celebration. Enticing Italian aromas wafted from the kitchen out into the dark dining room. I ordered scallops because that's what my mother ordered when she dined out. A magnum of wine sat on the table in front of me. I didn't like wine but drank it anyway. The scallops remained largely untouched, and I continued to sip away because I was nervous. The wine turned out to be an icebreaker with my new co-workers, who found tipsy me amusing, and we had a marvelous time laughing and talking, with me saying silly things in my shy way, and that evening paved the way to close friendships. One colleague told me she couldn't believe I was for real. I'm not sure what that meant, but I was what I was in all my unique and bountiful ineptitude.

However, friendship aside and without hesitation, two of my slyest co-workers asked if they could have Cher next time as their client. As hopelessly naive as I was, and I was pretty hopeless, I said no. They were a lot savvier and career focused than me, and the next time would be the last time she'd be mine.

Cher came to the shop, initially, by first having an associate call on the phone to announce her arrival. That was a little Hollywood. I was the esthetician; that's how she came to be my client. I had no time to get nervous, because I had to prepare the room and turn on the machines, and that I actually knew how to do. She walked in alone, quietly, and remained silent. She was quiet, and so was I. It was all very professional. She didn't show any personality, she didn't say anything, her face was a deadpan mask, so she was hard to describe to curious friends and co-workers. They felt let down. The procedure began with delicious cleansing cream, natural brushes, and gentle steam. Exfoliation and hand massage followed. I took my time. The facial was completed with a bracing astringent and toning masque. People's skin felt spanking brand new and pampered. Clients remarked that I gave the best facial ever; it's true. I did. This was something

I was well trained to do, and I knew how to do it, but Cher didn't say anything. Her skin was clear and taut.

Soon, she called me again, and I was thrilled. The relationship remained quiet and professional—same thing, she didn't say anything, and neither did I. But I would go to her, to the places where she was staying. The glamorous pop star generously gave me tickets to her play and, without the slightest reservation, let me take a photo of her sans makeup in her three-story penthouse hotel suite on the West Side. She asked what I was doing for Easter. "Oh, going home to visit, and have a big dinner." I couldn't think of anything else to say. Maybe I should have invited her, but I was too shy to be friendly. I would share the photo and story with my family. In the photo, just an ordinary snapshot, Cher displays the expression of a woman who has seen it all. She's looking directly at me with the tiniest, hardly visible *La Gioconda* smile. Her bare face looks great. I gave her a facial.

A wall of her suite was lined with many gorgeous shopping bags, glorious, expensive-store stuff. Wow. She could afford to shop like that. It seemed she had a bag from every store on Madison Avenue. Her two young, very fair, blonde children and sister came into the room and said hello. Little Elijah Blue favored blonde, blue-eyed Dad. He looked at me wide-eyed as he continued to talk very intelligently to his mom, and he appeared exceptionally bright. Cherilyn Sarkisian La Piere seemed like a good mother, very direct and centered, and she seemed to be a person who would be a safe friend.

I went to the play and took Andrew with me. Cher gave a wonderful performance and stood out on the stage. Andrew wasn't particularly moonstruck and thought the play stank. Apparently, others agreed, because it had a short run.

The multi-career entertainer, or her associate, would call when she needed her eyebrows shaped or bikini line waxed. Again, in silence, I would help pull off her form-fitting jeans that revealed slender thighs, a flat belly, and tiny underpants. A thin layer of hot wax was applied with a wooden tongue depressor and then quickly, firmly pulled off in the opposite direction of the hair growth. It hurt but just for a moment. I would gently pat the sensitive skin to lessen the sting. Throughout the procedure, she never flinched, never uttered a word or showed a flicker of emotion. She asked me to wax her entire face. I was appalled. "Won't that hurt?" I asked knowing that it would.

"It's okay," she assured me.

Apprehensive, I asked, "Won't it leave your skin red and blotchy?" knowing that it would, probably for days.

"It's okay," she said. "I do it all the time."

"Well, okay," I said, wondering why she did it, and hoped not to damage the famous face. I dipped the tongue depressor in the hot green wax and applied it to a small section of her face, starting at the side and proceeded to work quickly: dip, apply, rip. I moved from section to section: dip, apply, rip. From the sides to the lip: dip, apply, rip. From the lip to chin: dip, apply, rip. To the temples, across the forehead, working around the brows: dip, apply, rip. It was done. I applied a

soothing cream and another to remove any traces of wax. She
was satisfied, and I left, chagrined, wondering what a strange
thing I did to earn a living.

Cher stayed with Gene Simmons of Kiss, America's num-
ber-one gold record award-winning group of all time, at his
penthouse on the corner of Fifth Avenue in the 60s. I saw him
so briefly that I couldn't remark on Jill's appraisal of his appearance. The penthouse was a palace, with marble floors,
sumptuous fabrics, and an endless open-floor plan and views
of the park. Cher lounged on a plush chaise, the Queen of the
Nile. Apparently, she wanted me to move something and ges-
tured with her long hands. I was slightly put off and felt like
a servant. The apartment was warm and inviting, and something delicious was roasting in the oven. The air was fragrant
with the promise of a good meal. Hungry, I finished my work
and went out into the cold twilight, feeling like a handmaid.
The damp winter night hit me like a smart slap on the face.
Why should I be vassal, cipher, nonentity, to that television
goddess who dressed in feathers like the great ruined con-
tender and poor soul Mountain Rivera in *Requiem for a
Heavyweight*? I tried shaking the feeling off but felt stung
that, financially, I truly was poor. How could people be that
rich? I asked myself as I trudged to the subway that would
whisk me back to the shabby East Village. Cher sold millions
of records and had had one of the most enduring careers of
the century. I, a little Perth Amboyian, felt small indeed, very
small and little, but talked myself into an air of false superi-
ority. I was young and free from the entanglements of fortune

and fame, even though I much preferred the safety, elegance, and luxury of her Upper East Side digs to my very, very humble circumstances. They really weren't hers. She lived in an *Architectural Digest* Egyptian-fantasy dwelling in California. The penthouse was the kingdom of Mr. Kiss, and who knew what that was like?

The singer-actress-performer-personality paid promptly after services rendered and always tipped. Sometimes she paid by check. On one check, *Cher* was printed on the top, no last name, and the address of a Beverly Hills accountant; on another, just *Cher, The Chase Manhattan Bank, Park Avenue, New York, NY*. The date is 1982. In *Pay To The Order Of*, she wrote my first name only, just like hers. Her signature is chic and distinctive. I cashed the checks. *Pauper, Servus, Humilis*.

Except for the time on stage when she was costumed as a waitress, I never saw her dressed up or wearing makeup. She wore jogging attire, a good-quality pink jogging suit with white running shoes. Cher drank Perrier from the bottle in little sips and snacked on gold fish crackers. She never offered me a drink or snack, but she wasn't playing hostess—even though my mother had taught me not to eat in front of others unless you offer them something, too. Though only eleven years my senior, at the time, she seemed ages apart, serious and mature.

The Academy Award-winning actress seemed very normal and a lot more down-to-earth than I. In my own head, and in my head only, I was something of an artist and downtown

celebrity, such a silly young person. There was no end to my
foolishness, conceit, and self-centeredness—not at that age.
Cher was taller and bigger boned than me. We both had long
dark hair and were slender. Marc was incorrect; I didn't look
like her. I can't say that she looked rich, but she was a million
times, many millions of times, richer than I.

In high school, I'd had a crush on Gregg Allman, the lead
singer, organist, and songwriter for the Allman Brothers Band
and Cher's husband twice, but we had both moved on. I had
seen him at a concert in Jersey City up close, very close, so I
understood the attraction. I loved the Allman Brothers, too.

Somewhere along the way, while working with the fashion
icon, I had been interviewed at Fifty-fifth Street by *Women's
Wear Daily* to discuss the new skin-care line and services provided at the recently renovated shop. We spoke in my room
with closed doors, and I wasn't nervous. I talked about tech-
niques and products and mentioned Cher as a client, but when
the article appeared as a long column in the publication, it
mistakenly used the name Liza Minelli. My co-workers and
I were perplexed and disappointed, and I didn't bother to keep
even one copy of the incorrect article.

At about the same time, I had been featured on newly in-
novated Manhattan Cable Television, doing a makeover on a
young woman, so I was really getting to be a gal about town.
The director of the video wasn't overly enthusiastic with my
performance and insisted I use more makeup, both on the
model and me. We featured a natural look. "You're too
washed out! More color on the cheeks!" It was hot under

the lights, and we had an audience. No matter how much makeup I used, it wasn't enough to suit the director. "More color!" It was a long, frustrating experience, and I never saw the finished results, but by the time I was done, we, the model and I, both looked liked hot, tired, sad clowns, *Pagliacci*. That was the beginning and end of my television career. The only person I know who saw the tape was a policeman from Perth Amboy. He told me about it years later as I stood in the unemployment line, and I cringed.

Beauty is not a key to happiness. At age forty-nine, I hope to be a beautiful old woman. To be a naturally beautiful old lady requires at least pretty hair and soft skin. I'd rather go the Georgia O'Keefe or former socialite Mrs. Edith *Grey Gardens* Bouvier Beales way to natural aging beauty than the plastic surgeon's route, simply because I'd rather look old than look old and vain and maybe ridiculous. I've decided to look like Jane Goodall or George Smiley: nice, with a kind face and soft gray hair. On television, some seventy-plus actresses look quite shockingly taut, pulled way too tight. After seeing an Academy Award-winning, very rich, fitness-guru actress in Central Park, a friend noted the actress looked like "a fake teenager." That seemed sad. Why be a fake? Why not be a marvelous-looking old lady with white as snow hair and softly, gently aged skin, sweetness, and the sense to laugh at a silly old world, a lovely Lady Slane?

A keen observer of beauty from a young age, I hoped to be an artist, a painter. Instead, I worked as a makeup artist in my early twenties and saw many an aging beauty, actress, and stage star. Some looked happy, some not. On casual shopping trips, legendary singer and Tony and Grammy Award-winner Lena Horne wore no makeup and a trench coat. She was called one of the most beautiful women in the world. The exuberant, long-legged dancer Ann Miller was always well painted, eye lashed, and lacquered, which takes a tremendous amount of effort. She was in terrific form and highly spirited. We almost expected her to break into song and tap, as she had in the museum scene of *On the Town*, such was her buoyancy. Actress Dina Merrill, daughter of the Marjorie Merriweather Post and Edward F. Hutton fortunes, had enviable slimness and good hair, a great combination of natural assets enhanced by E. F. Hutton, I presume. She looked like money. Actress Geraldine Chaplin was the thinnest celebrity I ever saw, but when your grandfather is Eugene O'Neill, and your parents are Oona and Charlie, and you're Tonya in *Doctor Zhivago*, you surely must know more than a wee handmaid like me. Food is too delicious to be sacrificed for the sake of being skeletal.

Working with the clients required patience, lots and lots of patience, the patience of a mature person. Some patrons would spend an hour looking for a single lipstick. The dozens of lipsticks were named after New York addresses: Sutton Place, Beekman, Park Avenue, Wall Street, Chinatown. No lipstick was named for any East Village location, although there was a Washington Square. I worked six days a week, Monday through Saturday, and freelanced to pay my rent and grew tired, tired of temperamental actresses and actors who always seemed to be acting.

The red-bobbed chanteuse Karen Ackers walked in. I sneezed. "May I help you?" I asked.

"I'm singing tonight. I need someone else to wait on me!" she said, imagining I had a cold. I didn't. If I had been wise (I most assuredly was not), I would have let it go. Instead, I lost my temper. "Why don't you wrap yourself in a bubble!" I spewed and stormed away past stunned co-workers. When she performed at Café Carlyle, I didn't go.

In no particular order, here's a list of the people I met at the shop on Fifty-fifth Street: Catherine Deneuve, Mary Travers and her daughters, Buffy Sainte-Marie, Bill Beutell, Celeste Holmes, Margaret Hamilton, The Village People, Alison Steele, Rita Moreno, Richard Thomas, Colleen Dewhurst, Ashford & Simpson, Jerry Orbach, Ronnie Spector, Lorna Luft, Sylvia Miles, Lauren Bacall, the makeup artists for Kiss (who bought boxes of makeup—to wait on them meant a big commission), dancers from the American Ballet Theater, singers from the Metropolitan Opera, an Italian princess, heiresses, diplomats, and a slew of aspiring actresses hoping to get work on television commercials. I spoke to Carol Channing on the phone once, too.

Mary Travers and her daughters were very likeable. She was just how I would have expected the 1960s folk singer to be, warm and friendly, and when I saw her on the street, she said hello. The two girls bounded about the shop like blonde sheep-dog puppies. The straight blonde hair flew. Mary's did, too. They lived close by, and I saw them often.

The only autograph I ever asked for was from Buffy Sainte-Marie. Why? I don't know. I didn't know her work as a singer, songwriter, activist, or educator, she wasn't a household name, but she was approachable and kindly, and looked like a gentle hippy, though it wasn't that either. It had something to do with Mills and the competitor. They liked her. Maybe I was getting it for them in an effort to make right the wrong of the past. In my mind, buried under years of hidden hurt, was I trying to smooth out time and make concessions by getting an offering from a high priestess of the peace movement? Sometimes, I would wake up in the morning startled to recall a dream featuring someone I had thought long gone and forgotten—funny how people remain in the subconscious. The autograph is one of the few mementos of those days, other than my business card, and some photographs, that I still have.

As a young, twenty-something-year-old, I didn't know who acclaimed actress Colleen Dewhurst—her best known role was Marilla Cuthbert in *Anne of Green Gables*, or silver-screen siren, stage actress, and wife of Humphrey Bogart Lauren Bacall were, but Jean, the manager, always filled me in on who was who, and I made a note. Usually, I called my mother and asked her, too. All these years later, Ms. Bacall's husky voice still rings in my head, and thanks to classic films, many years after meeting them, I got to see these actresses on screen. Other memorable voices, of course, were the smoldering one of "Come, fly with me," radio deejay Alison Steele, "The Nightbird" and Broadway's comic actress Carol Channing.

Singers and songwriters Nick Ashford and Valerie Simpson beamed. Jean gushed, "Oh, he's so tall, dark, and handsome! Look at his curls!" He was indeed, tall, and she so petite. They both had dazzling smiles. When he smiled at Jean, her knees buckled.

Margaret Hamilton, a former schoolteacher, best known for her role as the green-skinned Wicked Witch of the West— cavorting with those ghastly, winged monkeys, the stuff of childhood nightmares—and the equally awful Miss Gulch of Kansas (and television's Cora for a coffee commercial), seemed fast, small in stature, in and out, with her small purchase in hand. "I'll get you, my pretty, and your little dog, too." No, she never uttered that famous line to us, but after she left, we had fun with it. One of the staff adeptly played the part, running around squealing.

Bill Beutell appeared presidential in his well-cut navy suit and big black waiting car; Celeste Holmes interfered with a co-worker's sale, causing her to lose it—she insisted you could by good quality brushes for less at the hardware store; The Village People seemed pleased with their success and were friendly and playful; Rita Moreno was tiny; Sylvia Miles seemed a typical New Yorker; Jerry Orbach was unassuming; and Richard Thomas was polite, just like John-Boy on *The Waltons*.

Lorna Luft, Judy Garland's second daughter, bolted into the shop ready for her appointment. The walls had just been painted a burnt orange. A vivacious performer, Ms. Luft flung her white fur coat over a short wall, also freshly painted, and I gasped. Apparently, it truly was quick-drying paint, though; no need to say a word.

Ronnie Spector, lead singer of the Ronettes and "the original bad girl of rock 'n' roll," came late for her appointment and slumped in my co-worker David's chair. I was hoping to say more than hello to the rocking robin, but she appeared tired, so I just had a look at the former Mrs. Phil Spector. By then, she had escaped from mad Phil (she describes all that in her bio). As I have mentioned, I met Phil in California with the Ramones. Cher began her career with a song called "Ringo I Love You" recorded by Spector. Ronnie recorded with, married, and divorced him. Much later in her career, bad girl was produced by Joey Ramone—and they became close friends—and recorded bad boy Johnny Thunders's ballad "You Can't Put Your Arms Around a Memory." Now, wouldn't it have been something if Cher and Ronnie—they were friends—had recorded with the Ramones? It's a small, rocking world. The day was ending; the session didn't go well. There was no repartee between Ronnie and the usual lady-charmer David. He was glad when it was over, and came out of his room mumbling under his breath.

Fame must be unpleasant. Catherine Deneuve, the French actress, was called the most beautiful woman in the world. Best known in this country as the face of Chanel No 5 perfume, her image drew attention to television screens and department store cosmetics counters, and Chanel's sales soared.

When she did those commercials, expert hair and makeup and light and film people provided their skills. After that came touch-ups on still photographs. She wore beautiful gowns. The stage was set for perfection. When she quietly came in the shop, she appeared a middle-aged woman with a hauntingly sad expression. We were curious to see her. *Belle de Jour* seemed shy, pointed more than she spoke, and selected a pretty pink-gold eye shadow. She came back the following day to make another small purchase. Miss Deneuve's had thick blonde hair, wore a lavender suit, and carried a lavender handbag. Hmmm, so that's how French movie-stars dress, I noted. One of my male co-workers said, "Gee, she's heavier than I thought." No one on the street would have turned around and said, "Look at that heavy woman," though. She wasn't. She was normal, not pencil thin and certainly not heavy, just average, so she didn't live up to the screen image my co-workers had in mind, because it would have been impossible.

Director-actor Woody Allen and paramour-actress Mia Farrow came in, but I was in the back working. "Why didn't you call me to come out, Jean?" I asked my friend the manager. Jean looked after me and didn't want me to miss anything. People were constantly telling me I looked like Mia. I heard it so often, it irked me. I thought she was kind of kooky. Was she pretty? I would have liked being told I looked like Greta Garbo, but I wasn't because I didn't. I looked like my father and mother. *Vanity of vanities; all is vanity.* It's all fleeting. It all passes. There's a church in Rome that is adorned with the skulls and bones of Capuchin monks through the ages. Soon enough, we'll all look like them.

The most memorable person I met via the shop was Lieutenant Governor of New York Mario Cuomo. First, important, serious men who looked like FBI agents in dark suits entered the shop. Through a series of conversations, they asked how to go about engaging a service. Lieutenant Governor Cuomo was going to appear on television to announce his run for the governorship and needed help concealing the dark circles under his eyes. That was going to be a challenge. I offered my expertise and agreed to go to the hotel, not really knowing how to conceal what needed to be corrected by a plastic surgeon. Now, this wasn't mere vanity. The governor had very distracting bags under his eyes. I consulted our top makeup expert, and he advised me. I went to the Lexington Avenue hotel dressed very appropriately in a blouse and skirt and armed with heavy duty, medical-procedure concealer in many shades, foundations, powders, and brushes. A large dark man opened the door. He reminded me of my uncle, who had been murdered. He took one look at a very young, petite me, and was most kind, most gentlemanly. He took the time to ask about life on East Fifth Street and the Third Street Hell's Angels, and he took the time to listen to my answer. "Well," I hesitated. "The Hell's Angel's don't seem to bother anyone. In fact, residents feel they act as our crime watch, so they're a bonus in the neighborhood." He seemed to understand. There was little light in the hotel room, so he suggested we use the bathroom, where the lights were strong. I performed my services as best as I could, with him sitting on the only available seat, the toilet. His ladylike wife, elderly mother, and children were all present. I felt comfortable with the family. His mother reminded me of my grandmother in her black dress and white hair. His kids, Andrew, Chris, and the girls, were my age, and everyone was nervous and dressed up for the big TV event. My work was probably not spectacular, but he was a warm and gracious man. We shook hands all the way around, and I departed and went back to work and called my mother to tell her what a lovely man he was. "He's a Democrat," she said. "*Presto, sui! Mario! Mario!*" That was a one-time deal. I never saw him again, and it took me months to get paid, but it was a wonderful experience.

Besides the celebrities, many clients were all-American type young women, who needed black-and-white headshots for their acting auditions; usually that meant television commercials. The mostly young hopefuls came to have their makeup expertly applied before a photograph. One not-as-young woman came frequently, whenever she had an audition. Slender and of medium height, her fashionable blonde hair was well coiffed, but she was in no way outstanding, and her teeth were flawed. She spent her days at acting, voice, and dance lessons and various beauty appointments. Perhaps not particularly bright, she was smart enough to live at a cushy address with an older man who paid the bills. As far as we knew, she never landed a job, and we never saw her on television. She did appear in the shop, however, wearing many different fur coats.

Once, a big man with a wide frame came in and asked if I could wax his back. The thought made me want to run out the door. Instead, I pulled the owner aside and asked him. With raised eyebrows and a frown, he said, "You don't have to if you're uncomfortable." The owner was slightly apprehensive. I was uncomfortable. It could have been difficult, even expose us to liability issues, so I politely refused, saying the shop didn't offer that service. When he left, I sank into my chair, thankful for having an understanding boss.

Jean, the manager, and my very dear friend, asked me to wax the crevice in her behind. "It'll be nice and cool for the summer," she explained.

I was utterly floored. "No, Jean! No!" I said without any hesitation. "That'll hurt too much. I can't do it."

Jean asked our co-worker and very dear friend Lana.

"Jean, are you nuts? What if you get an infection?" Lana replied.

Jean turned her back, closed the door, and did it herself.

By the way, the most demanding, obnoxious clients were, hands down, Long Island housewives. It was always frustrating when a customer, a woman, would prefer having a man wait on her. We had a man working with us part time on Saturdays. Ira knew and pretended to know nothing about cosmetics, yet the women would wait in order for him to wait on them. He practiced as a psychotherapist during the week but worked at the Fifty-fifth Street salon on Saturdays to get free shampoo. He was intense looking, with an almost bald head and trim beard, but we had fun in and out of the shop. Ira threw a good party with champagne at his Upper West Side digs and invited the whole staff. Andrew came, too, of course, wearing his trademark black-leather pants. I wore gold lamé jeans, and Ira, who was gay, said I had the best backside in New York City. It looked to me like that of a shiny young mare. It was high and round and stuck out too much on my small frame. I didn't like it. At best it resembled that of a Rococo cherub on the ceiling of a beautiful Sicilian church, at worst a balloon. *Balloon Dog.*

Ira knew how to have fun and exhibited great *joie de vivre*. He rented a schooner with friends for a weeklong Caribbean bacchanal. It was the most fantastic idea I ever heard: sun, warm breezes, and days on a boat under sail. I wanted to be one of the boys and go, too, but it was an all-male escapade.

A madwoman patronized the shop. Norma wore pale foundation, penciled in eyebrows, and orange-red lipstick. She dashed into the shop, asked for a lipstick, and admonished us, "You all look like whores! Wash that makeup off your faces! Jeez, just like that one Brooke Shields." Then she'd be gone. I didn't mind her. She knew what she wanted and didn't waste anyone's time.

Maybe Norma had been right. For years, it took one solid hour to apply my makeup. The face had to be properly cleansed and moisturized with three products and pure cotton balls, and then the procedure began with Max Factor pancake makeup and a natural sea sponge squeezed to the correct degree of dampness. The sensational pancake makeup left a perfect matte finish on the face and lips. The skin was a bisque fresco, a blank canvas. Concealer went under the eyes. At twenty-something, I had nothing to conceal, but I did it anyway. Then I was ready to go with sable makeup brushes and flat containers containing color. After the foundation, I applied loose powder with a large, fluffy brush to "set" the makeup, followed by a light brown powder and special brush to contour the face. I had plenty of bone structure, high Russian cheekbones from my father and high Italian cheekbones from my mother, so it wasn't necessary, but it was a chance to apply more stuff and use another brush. Next came the subtle colored powders for cheeks and eyes, one color on the cheek and one to highlight, three colors on the eyes: base, contour, highlight, and three more brushes. The real work began by lining the eyes with black kohl, upper and lower and the inside rim. Mascara followed, combed out with a gold-plated utensil to avoid lumps. For special occasions (then, as it had with Ann Miller, it became every day), I used false eyelashes. That was tricky. The eyelashes, either on a strip or individual lashes, were quickly attached with an adhesive. I completed the look with lip liner, lipstick applied with a lip brush, and lip gloss. I didn't go out the door until all that was done. My *maquillage* was kept in a big black professional makeup case that looked like a fish tackle box, filled to the rim with goodies.

The shop had established its reputation by selling theatrical makeup, one of the few places in New York City to continue to do so. Showcased were interesting things like stage blood, latex and crepe hair, and grease paint. Grease paint came in a tube like oil paint and had a distinct smell and texture. There wasn't much call for theatrical grease paint in the 1980s. It seemed like a survival of the James Tyrone era of stage acting; nonetheless, it gave the place a sense of continuity and theatricality, and being located within short distance of many great stages, it was appropriate and old New York. There wasn't much need for pancake makeup, either, but the store held on to those traditional items as a matter of principle.

"Television Face Lift" came in a small pink box. It was a plastic kit that contained adhesive squares and some elastic bands. It could be used to pull the face up, and then the tape and bands were concealed under a wig. There wasn't much demand for that product, but we stocked the boxes on a corner shelf. Once in a while, an old man would buy a few, and I would turn from him and silently giggle. I was proud of the shop.

Eventually, most of my co-workers left to start their own businesses. One of the gals sells her private-label brand on television infomercials and owns a mid-town shop. Lana was a natural-born saleswoman. She'd pick up her dress from the dry cleaners, hang it in her workspace, and then sell it at a profit to the customer in her chair. She could sell anything to anyone and had commissions and bonuses to prove it. Clients didn't leave her chair without buying hundreds of dollars' worth of makeup. Surprisingly, they were always happy to do so. Lana made everyone feel as if each was her best, best friend, and clients left the shop hugging and kissing her, laughing, as large bags were carted to waiting chauffeur-driven cars. But then, after the big sale, they would call her, their brand-new friend on the phone, with a long list of annoying questions like, What do I do with this brush? And this one? And where does this color go? And how come it doesn't look like it did when I left the shop?

I, too, fell for Lana's gregarious nature. We were good friends and often had fun together. For a while, fed up with guys, we decided to treat ourselves the way we wished to be treated and ventured to a swanky restaurant. We arrived, two dressed-up twenty-somethings, ordered chateaubriand and wine for our feast, and had a swell time, probably enjoying the experience more than the couples who surrounded us. Sometimes, we'd go out for ice-cream sundaes. Lana had a full-figured, voluptuous shape, and I was still less than a hundred pounds. She craved thinness, but it was not to be. She was lovely in her own way but couldn't accept it. "I'd trade with you, Lana, if I could," I said. I didn't see the great merit of thinness. She looked at me and continued to eat with real gusto. She truly loved food.

The Fifty-fifth Street shop owner's wife frightened me. She never did anything, but she frightened me just the same. Of course, most people did, so it was nothing out of the ordinary. Lana, however, really despised the woman and claimed the feeling was reciprocal. They couldn't have been more opposite. Kate was thin, plain, and from the Midwest. Lana was

Sephardic, with exotic eyes, olive skin, and dark hair, and had grown up in the Bronx. When people said Lana looked like Liza Minelli, she exploded. It's usually not a good idea to make such comments, unless the person of note is positively breathtaking. Kate was reserved; Lana was effervescent. "Oh, she's such a WASP!" Lana would groan. I had never heard that term before. I don't think Kate loved Lana, but for business reasons she put up with her. One day their mismatched personalities collided. Lana had left her lunch, a huge, fragrant pastrami sandwich, leaking from the brown paper bag on the counter by the cash register. Kate walked past, picked up the bag with the tips of her fingers and held it at arm's length. She pinched her nose and demanded, "*What* is *this?*" Mortified, Lana's face turned red, and she wished to crawl under the counter.

Miss Lana could have done stand-up comedy. She was a natural comic actress. Her opening line, "I'm your makeup artist of *love!* What fabulous Nefertiti eyes you have!" She sparkled with amusing monologue, facial expressions, and exuberant body language, and put on quite a show, client after client, until the end of the day, when she collapsed. Talented, hardworking Lana was worthy of a Tony of her own. She appears on television once in a while, selling away.

Lana focused on making big bucks. She tried for years without success to become a union makeup artist, which involved a certain amount of politics, but she just didn't have the elusive connection. A former co-worker did, and that woman moved on to network news and did the makeup for the most famous, highest-paid female anchor. Lana got really worked up when she saw that former co-worker's name in the credits of the hour-long program every week. "She's not that good," she muttered in distress. Once in a while, Miss-Not-that-Good would come to the shop looking like a million. She was tall and slim and immaculately well groomed, like a model, and that ruined Lana's day.

Things turned out bleaker for Jean. She was held up at gunpoint once, then again. The first time, I was in the shop, but in back with a client in my room, unaware of what was happening. When I came out, I was told. Jean seemed strong and unshaken. She had given the thug the money, and he'd fled to the corner and into the subway. "I'm okay," she assured us. The second time, she had been sexually violated, too. I had resigned by then and wasn't living in New York. That second time, she was deeply affected. She fled New York for Hawaii and left her marriage. The last news I had was that she was living in Brooklyn and working in a factory, and I never heard from or about her again. Jean was a warm, kind-hearted soul, and a survivor. In her Ohio hometown, she had worked for the town's richest man, a mortician and pimp. She'd escaped that for New York City. Her husband was good-natured, too, but the two childhood friends had tired of each other and grown apart. Jean had a fantasy about rowing him out to the middle of the Central Park Lake. He had a compulsion to jump into deep water, though he couldn't swim. I thought replacing his toothpaste with anchovy paste in a tube would be fun. We never did either. Meanwhile, she had taken up with a singer from the Reverend James Cleveland's gospel chorus and was enthralled by her new love. Motherly Jean would bring me food to work and insist on providing cab fare when I visited her at home on the Upper West Side. She took me out for chicken, ribs, and cornbread, and called me Miss Bunny.

At the shop, we had gotten a new item, small blocks of rice powder packaged in little, square gold boxes with a picture of an Asian girl on the cover. "She looks like you, Miss B.," Jean said, and she sparked an idea. Miss Bunny had a black satin dress with a slit and a big straw coolie hat bought at one of the tiny Chinatown stores. For a party, Bunny dressed and made up as the girl on the box, with white skin and red lips and her straight black hair. We took photos. Jean loved them and framed one to keep on her dresser. I kept one, too.

A group photo of the staff, standing behind the counter of the shop, shows Jean with deep bronze skin, golden wavy hair, and a wide smile on her coral lips—a golden girl with a heart of gold.

More gold was to come. The title "Royal Esthetician" replaced Miss Bunny. Clients, the most exotic and beautiful creatures, gentle and kind, arrived from the Royal Government of Bhutan, the Buddhist Himalayan kingdom. Graciously and unexpectedly, they presented the Royal E with a red-velvet-and-gold-embossed book of stamps from the Post and Telegraphs Department of Bhutan. The book contains gold, red, and green medallions of their ruler, a young and handsome boy king. Several pages contain three-dimensional stamps of Renoir still lifes and van Gogh's *Sunflowers*, as well as Bhutanese dragons, animals, Michelangelo's *David*, Greek and Roman art, and Bhutanese teapots. Included is a post card from the country famous for monasteries and majestic mountains, most notably Everest.

The store manager who preceded Jean—we didn't care for her—married a celebrated screen actor who often played psychologically unstable characters, and she herself became a character actor and very successful casting agent. She came in to gloat once in a while and tell us about things Hollywood. Ho-hum, we said after she left. Coincidentally, this well-known actor lived next door to Fairfield James's mother. Mrs. So-and-So had two of the actor's kittens that she used to catch mice. I doubt if she fed them, and James gave me photos of the two gray kittens. Sometimes, it's a small world, indeed.

As for actors, I only knew one, Vincent. He was younger than I, and I wasn't interested in him. He worked as a dish-washer at a place called Evelyn's Kitchen, next to the Ninth Precinct. It was a dark and smoky bar down a short flight of stairs where a French woman cooked delicious food: leeks vinaigrette, and mussels in white wine. Jill and Suzy both thought he was cute, and Suzy was crazy over him, but I couldn't figure him out. He was so unusual, neat and clean in a *film noir* way, almost from a different time and place. In a city with many striving for originality, he didn't have to try; he just was a true original and looked rather like a young Kirk

Douglas. A prominent chin dominated his bony face; the jaw thrust out, and he was skinny and slight, not much bigger than me, so strange in looks and personality. Jill said he was okay but full of himself and always broke.

I lived right down the street from Evelyn's, so he came to talk to me once in a while, we'd span a little time, and then I'd send him away. Jill claimed he had a huge crush on me, but I didn't notice. He liked my clothes. Vincent particularly liked the red wool pleated skirt that I wore to work. "So much better than leather," he said about the soft, school-girlish skirt. He told me good stories that made me laugh, but I never knew what to believe, what was tripe and what wasn't, and it didn't matter. Vincent said his family was the Gallo family, the mob family. I listened. He didn't want to be part of the family firm, so they were estranged. He was taking acting lessons with the great Stella Adler, so he said. The legendary acting coach would have been in her eighties. Meanwhile, I had to go to work.

Years later, Vincent appeared in a full-color spread in *Esquire*. Shortly after, there was Vincent, again, on television with his name listed in the credits. For a time, it seemed, whenever I picked up my head, there was Vincent looking back at me. After that, a co-worker and editor at a medical journal would tell me she'd seen a movie starring Vincent Gallo. "You're kidding," I said. "I knew that guy when he was a dishwasher."

Finally, many years after East Fifth Street, my husband and I saw *Buffalo 66*—written, directed, and starring Vincent

Gallo. We laughed; loved it, watched it again, and promised to watch it every year on Valentine's Day. "Fools rush in where angels fear to tread. . . ."

The summer of 1986, I enrolled at a summer semester program at Columbia University that included a theater class. It was great living at the Hartley Hall dorm and okay sharing a suite with five others. George and I became best pals. He was my favorite suitemate, a tall lanky Texan wild boy who'd come to New York for the summer class to have fun. His well-to-do parents (his father was a corporate lawyer and his mother owned radio stations) had sent him in the hopes that he might pursue an education, but the effeminate George was out to go to the clubs and see the sights. He never picked up a book or did any work other than swig back a beer first thing in the morning to go with the first of many cigarettes. He was ten years younger than I was, and would pull practical jokes like jump out of my closet after I went to bed or hang from the ledge of the building for laughs. I liked George, but he was so slow and poky that I'd be talking to him while we were walking only to find he was half a block behind me, smoking, with his head in the clouds. We had a History of New York class in the morning—taught by a professor voted as one of the ten best in America. "New York has everything you want and everything you don't want," he said. The class was followed by an afternoon walking tour and lunch at an interesting or landmark restaurant.

The day we toured the area north of the campus, I didn't

feel well, so George escorted me back to the suite. There was a shoot-out at the famed soul-food restaurant. Our suitemates came back all excited. No one had been hurt, it was just something to tell the folks back home, but we'd missed the big event.

Dressed in a white-and-navy striped sweater, white skirt, white patent-leather Fiorucci heels with a black patent tie in back, and white lacy hose I wasn't sure about but it was getting late and I had no other stockings, George insisted we go to dinner at the restaurant at the Trump Tower. It was something he was keen to do, and he dressed up in a suit and tie and polished loafers. His hair was neatly slicked back instead of the teased and matted wild nest it was most of the time. After the unmemorable meal at the glitzy restaurant, after a quick sightseeing trip to the lobby of the morbid Chelsea Hotel, again, George's childish desire where he delighted in the bizarre characters who graced the place, and a fast (for Texas Jorge) drink in the gloomy bar next door, we joined the class at the Public Theater to see *Vienna Lusthaus*. In the theater's minimal lobby, Jackie Onassis was huddled in a corner, dangling a paper coffee cup between her legs in a rather slouched position, not at all the way one would expect to see the most famous, most touted, most photographed woman in the world. Accompanying her was companion, Maurice Templesman. I was directly across from her and close enough to see her heavy mascara and smooth skin and blank expression.

I looked at her, and she looked at me. Then she took a long look at my questionable hose. I wondered what she thought, wished I hadn't worn them, and wanted to tear them off. Bare legs would have been better. She used a lot of hair spray. She looked at me again, and I looked at her. She looked at my legs, while I looked at her hair and face—a quiet exchange between two women. Her appearance was unremarkable until she stood up. Then she was transformed. She was a large, big-boned woman, equestrian in appearance. Her clothes were plain but superbly tailored and fit her like a glove. She had no lines, no crinkles, nothing bunched, no tummy. Her clothes seemed to be made of super-fine, super-high tech, second-skin fabric that held everything in perfect place, Superwoman clothes not from this planet. She wore a black-and-white striped shirt, black trousers, black heels, and carried a noticeably expensive bag with an ornamental clasp. On her wrist dangled an ivory bangle bracelet. The shirt, belt, trousers, even the hose and black high heels, seemed to be one seamless piece, a jumpsuit made from the finest, softest girdle-like fabric. The shirt would never untidily peek out of the pants. The black hose would not bunch at the ankle. The theater buzzed. She presented a spectacularly more interesting performance than whatever was on stage. Twenty some years later, not a single moment of *Vienna Lusthaus* comes to mind.

After the play, she walked slowly, with perfect carriage, through the crowd, looking straight ahead, like an all-knowing queen of the universe. A newspaper photographer popped up and snapped her picture with blinding flashes. It was awful. She just kept walking straight ahead, seemingly without blinking an eye or moving the well-sprayed hair, to her waiting car, followed by the unobtrusive Mr. Templesman. When we returned to the dorm, the students called home to relay the Jackie sighting to pleased parents, happy to know their children had been in rarified company for the evening and their money well spent.

(As an aside, Jackie looked best as Mrs. O, with her long dark hair, oversized shades, and black leather trench coat. It's been many a year since the masses have participated in such a world-class, world-stage spectacle as the triangle between Jackie, he-devil Ari, and that most dramatic Greek goddess, the fantastically divine Madame Callas. Maria's face, voice, passion, and talent, her life was a work of tragic and gloriously triumphant art. Maria shone brightest of all the stars in the entire firmament, the alpha-and-omega. There will never be another Maria *Vissi d'arte* Callas. See Pasolini's *Medea* for Maria the Great.)

In the late 1980s, through "Hey, Uptight Old Mr. Normal" and his brother, Len, came the remarkable acquaintance of a Mr. Ben Schmidt. Herr Schmidt was a rare individual, and I don't expect to meet another like him again. He was one of a kind and a truly marvelous person. Mr. Schmidt was unique. His physical appearance astounded. Heads turned, even in New York; people turned to stare at him. When in his company, strangers asked if he was my bodyguard. Ben was a giant of a man: tall and of enormous girth—Falstaffian in size, but noble in character. Of course, I never asked his weight, but he may have been more than three hundred pounds. He was a big Black Irish fellow with dark hair and dark eyes. When I was in church once with him, an old woman behind me tapped my shoulder and gushed, "He's the handsomest man I've ever seen!"

Not everyone who met Schmidt was so enamored. People either loved him or didn't. He was intimidating. He had strong, extreme, very unpopular political views that he was not shy about sharing in mixed company. He was a complete idealist and made many enemies, sometimes powerful enemies.

The first time I met him was at the home of "Uptight." Ben was spewing forth about an historical event, something regarding the Hapsburg dynasty. I didn't know what he was talking about. He was like an impassioned college professor with an encyclopedic mind, ranting to an audience of three. I was very quiet at that meeting.

We had lobster for lunch, and Mr. Schmidt didn't know how to eat it. I felt sorry for him, and later sent him instructions in the mail. A man of such knowledge should not have been in that embarrassing position again.

Sometimes a minute act of kindness can stir up all kinds of emotions in someone of the opposite sex, especially someone without much experience, and that's what happened. Dear Mr. Schmidt fell madly in love with me and would have gone to the ends of the earth to win my love and affection. I was fond of him but, sadly, never fell in love with the kindly, generous gent. He made weekly marriage proposals, and I refused. He was a whirlwind, and when he entered the room, all the air went out.

After the relationship with "Uptight," the always-chival-
rous Schmidt stepped up to the mound. With his giant presence came gifts of all kinds: flowers, chocolates, and
extravagant nights on the town. He knew I dearly loved New
York, and after I had moved from there, he was more than
happy to drive the hour to my home, and then drive the hour
to the city, and then do the reverse drive back. He researched
places to take me, and he always did a fine job. If I made a
suggestion, he was happy to deliver. We had tremendous fun,
and he had deep pockets. He was a seriously funny, talented
person. He should have been on the stage. He could sing and
act, and had charisma. People compared him to John Candy,
but he was more than the delightful Candy. He was compa-
rable to the great wit and writer G.K. Chesterton. However,
beneath all of his gifts, there was a deep insecurity. There
shouldn't have been, because he was a wonder, but there was.
He felt he had to outdo the lawyer who came before him.
"Uptight" was no great shakes, so Ben really didn't have to
work that hard. Among the many wonderful places we went
were the cabarets.

In the mid- to late-1990s, Annie Ross, a top-notch jazz
singer, performed at the Rainbow Room. In her sixties, she
looked terrifically slim in a slinky red gown that covered her
from the neck to the ankles. Barbara Cook sang at Café Carlyle, splendidly attired in the magnificence of her voice, and
Eartha Kitt donned a leopard print cat suit at the same venue.
At the end of the performance, Miss Kitt went around the
room, amicably shaking hands. To see these gals perform with

excellence and grace impressed me. Talent has no age. And let's not forget great jazz gents, septuagenarians and octogenarians all: Clark Terry, Marty Napoleon, Billy Taylor, Clem DeRosa, Freddy Cole, Lenny Argese, Earl May, Bucky Pizzarelli, Toots Thielman, and Perth Amboy's own "Moonlight" Sonata (*adagio sostenuto*) into "My Funny Valentine" Morris Nanton.

What Tiffany's is to Holly Golightly, the Carlyle Hotel is to me: a safe haven from the world in a stately building in a premier location. Not much bad could happen in that enclave of *luxe*. I did once witness a patron at the Café become vocal and testy when the coat attendant didn't produce his outerwear quickly enough. Other than that act of rudeness and being a little crowded in that room, though, I like the place. If I were rich, I'd live there. I'd move right in and not bother to take anything with me. There would be no need. All would be available with the touch of a fingertip. The hotel offers the best of everything ensconced in privacy and hushed refinement. The park and museums are close by, so there's plenty to do.

Kitty Carlisle Hart, best known as a panelist on *To Tell the Truth* for twenty years, performed on stage in her *nineties*. My husband and I said hello and were enormously taken by her charm. In a world gone sloppy, she was elegant in a flattering, slim, well-fitted green suit and smart low-heeled shoes, hair carefully coifed, and expert makeup. At age ninety, she was soft and had a terrific smile. She seemed immensely likeable, and her ladylike appearance hadn't altered all that much from *Night at the Opera*, nor had her singing. That was the last time I saw a really well-dressed woman. We saw her again, dressed casually for a short afternoon stroll in navy exercise pants and jacket, white sneakers, and the lovely smile, attended by a nurse-companion. She's a great example of looking wonderful at any age.

My old-world grandmother tied her fine-as-corn silk white hair in two braids and pinned them atop her head. She wore blue printed housedresses, an apron tied at the waist, and white Keds on her feet. I loved that look. It was simple, feminine, and practical. Her hands were soft and supple, smooth as olive oil, and she kept very slender. She drank sweet, milky coffee instead of eating food. I never saw her eat, but she excelled in cooking. If she had an occasion to leave the house, usually for a funeral, she wore, of course, a black dress, black veiled hat, a black coat, black shoes, stockings, and shoes. She was a humble woman without a trace of pretense. My grandmother had the same timeless dignity as the elders dressed in their best clothes at *Babette's Feast*. With their simply arranged white hair and austere garments, they are refined beyond compare.

The great Babette's words are engraved on my heart: "An artist is never poor."

> *The barge she sat in, like a burnish'd throne,*
> *Burn'd on the water; the poop was beaten gold;*
> *Purple the sails, and so perfumed that*

The winds were love-sick with them; the oars were silver,
Which to the tune of flutes kept stroke, and made
The water which they beat to follow faster,
As amorous of their strokes. For her own person,
It beggar'd all description.

—Antony and Cleopatra

7

THE BEATLES' INFLUENCE,

AND A BIG CHANGE

$\circ\!\!\!\sim$

SOMETIME IN THE 1950s, a Southern preacher, The Reverend Jimmy Snow, denounced rock 'n' roll as a bad influence on young people. He was mocked and ridiculed. Say what you will, he had a point. Drugs fueled by rock 'n' roll were the demise of so many peers. Perhaps they'd have been better off staying home and learning to play the violin and listening to Mozart, rather than searching the globe and licking the earth. My mother, quoting Shaw, would say, "Youth is wasted on the young." There's truth in that, too.

When I came up with a particularly stupid idea, my mother stayed quiet for a while and tried to reason with me. "Remember, I was young once, too," she said. Her high school yearbook photo shows a stunner with glossy curls and a knockout smile. She was a brunette version of a young Marilyn Monroe. A photo shows Mom in all her youthful glory standing along the railing by the waterfront. Someone had written *Legs!* on the bottom of the picture. Her legs were gorgeous, and she wears black pumps similar to the ones I bought at Ian's.

Calm was not really in my mother's nature. Her response to my more inane questions or requests was along the lines of, "Have you lost your *mind?*" but sometimes she would surprise me or just give up.

When I was seven years old, she allowed me to go to the movies with the big girls to see *A Hard Day's Night*. Permitting me to see the film was probably a big mistake, the biggest mistake of her life. My tender self was mesmerized, the music blew me away, the girls, the boys, were just so fantastic, who wanted to do anything or be anything but them? How could I continue being a little girl when I wanted to be a Beatle girl?

But my poor mom didn't know any of this, so I absolve her. After all, Frank Sinatra had enchanted her and many of her generation at a young age. From hearing "The Chairman of the Board" at home so often, I knew Sinatra as well as I would know The Beatles. I knew all about Nancy, the girl from Jersey City, and how he left her and the three children to pursue Ava Gardner. Ava ran with the bullfighters. Frank's career bottomed out, but he staged the comeback of the century and made *From Here to Eternity*. I kept quiet about the mob and knew the Rat Pack with Deano and Sammy Davis. Mia Farrow confounded me, too. I knew about tough old Dolly. I knew it all and knew Frank Sinatra better than I knew my own relations, because my mother didn't speak to many of them. My parents took us to Frank's old hometown, Hobo-

ken, where we had steamers in melted butter at the world famous Clam Broth House. This was in the old days, when saw-
dust covered the floors, a help-yourself clam broth dispenser
stood on the counter, and worn workingmen filled the bar. As
a rising star, Sinatra had come to my mother's high school—
the same school where I had the traumatic fight as a freshman—when she was a young student to do some political
campaigning in the 1940s.

Seated in that dark movie palace, the palatial Majestic
Theater, with thick red carpet under little feet, eager on the
plush red seat waiting for the heavy red velvet drapes to pull
away from the big screen to see *A Hard Day's Night*, my big
eyes became wide saucers and I flipped back my long black
braids. My mother always tied a ribbon on top of my head.
I was wearing a dress because little girls didn't wear pants as
much in those days.

When the film started, thrilled, I jumped up and down in
my chair and started to scream with the big girls. Who were
these fabulous boys with the beautiful hair, and how would I
meet and marry them? At age seven, Ringo was my favorite,
and analyzing it these forty-two years later, it was probably
because he smiled the most. The four Beatles looked like dolls,
playing their instruments, with their perfect hair, neat suits,
and little boots, and girls like dolls. And I loved the music,
and the early Beatles' stayed my favorite. I went through all
the phases with them, but the early days remained the best.

In many ways, I wish I never heard of The Beatles. They
were the first to break my heart, and they did it over and over

again. My heart broke when Paul didn't marry his girlfriend Jane. I couldn't forgive him. They broke my heart when their image changed from cute to the maharaja, and, again, when John and Cynthia's marriage ended, and once more, when they grew beards. The breakup was the last straw.

The old industrial port city of Perth Amboy was, in my young mind, not all that different from Liverpool, so the boys and I had something in common: we were Liver-Perth-pudlians, puddings, together. When my family and I went to the beach at Sandy Hook, we looked out at the Atlantic Ocean and whispered that, straight ahead, was England, Liverpool, Paul McCartney. The black-and-white film of *A Hard Day's Night* had the same grainy quality as the gritty texture of my hometown with its dry docks and dilapidated piers and river smells, tankers from foreign countries, old brick factories and smokestacks, refineries and refinery gases and odors, the once-bustling train station and city stores, taverns, and immigrant population with old-world faces like the Irish actor who played Paul's grandfather.

Unfortunately, I once had a relationship with someone who bore a striking resemblance to the Paul McCartney of 1964. Well, maybe it was more a *mezzogiorno* Paul, early-Elvis look: dark hair, dark eyes, tight pants. He was the hair-dresser who'd ruined my hair by dying it platinum. He was also the reason for meeting Bob McKenna of the NYPD's Ninth Precinct.

Our friend, an intelligent young stylist who had once worked at *Vogue* and later for MTV, introduced me to Andrew. Nita was educated, elegant, and chic in a slim, platinum way, although she did have a big crush on Iggy Pop, who seemed a surprising choice. (That's not to disparage Ig, who certainly deserves his rock 'n' roll acclaim for great stuff like "Lust for Life.") Her lovely older sister produced television commercials and had suggested to me to go to the place on Fifty-fifth Street for the job. Nita failed to tell me that Andrew had beaten his previous girlfriend, but eventually I would find that out myself.

There are always early indications, warning signs, red flags of what's to come in a relationship. Trust your instincts and loyal friends. If someone tells you something that doesn't make sense, something doesn't add up, it's probably because it's not true. Don't hope for the best. Accept things as they are, not what you want them to be, and you'll save yourself trouble. Unfortunately, I, little naïve Cabiria, wouldn't learn that for another twenty years—*le tourbillon da la vie* (the whirlwind of life).

Early in the courtship, Andrew invited me to brunch on a Sunday morning. We were going to meet at his apartment on lower Fifth Avenue. After ringing the intercom, I waited for a little too long. Out of the elevator stumbled a disheveled blonde in a black plastic trench coat. That should have been my first sign. I asked Andrew about it, but he knew nothing. Not long after, Jill, Daniel, Andrew, and I were at a club. Jill and Daniel drifted away, and my date Andrew did, too. I was left alone. Daniel came back and told me Andrew was outside with a girl. I confronted him when he showed up. Andrew denied it, and that should have been my second sign and the end. That about sums up Andrew's fidelity to our relationship.

I learned to be tough. Don't give anyone a second chance. One strike, and you're out. Years later, when I worked at a publishing company with a marvelous woman, Shirley Shalit (Gene's sister-in-law), her pearl was, "What you get before the marriage is what you get after the marriage." I wasn't about to get married, but Shirley's advice remains priceless.

Andrew and I did have something in common: Neither of us took drugs—no cocaine, no pills, and no big daddy heroin. He had seen too many Staten Island friends incarcerated or dead. Dope presented an expensive waste of time and money, and it destroyed your looks, and Andrew was way too vain to let that happen. Neither of us smoked anything, and we only had an occasional drink. Andrew didn't hold liquor well. His personality changed even after one drink, and not for the better.

As the relationship with Andrew progressed, I liked him less and less. He started looking less attractive, less like Paul McCartney and more like Eddie Munster. The hair became blacker and blacker and slicker and slicker. The pants became tighter and tighter, until they began to strangle him. We didn't get along. I grew to detest him and his ways. He was conceited and shallow, and spent way too much time arranging his inky hair and arching his thick eyebrows. Never did Narcissus pass by a mirror or store window without stopping to make an adjustment. He was lazy and not all that bright.

Andrew shoveled through the dirty clothes to find something clean to wear. He kept a long dead tree in his apartment. The leaves were all shriveled and black like old bananas. "Maybe it'll grow, again," he said without a care or thought in the world. When it was time for me to go to sleep, it was time for him to play guitar. We weren't in tune, ever, and were never going to be. He got on my nerves and drove me crazy. Daniel and Richard loathed him. Vince Gallo didn't like him or his clothes. "I saw you and Andrew on Broadway. You looked like rock stars," Vince said with disapproval. We did. I had a new white coat with black leopard spots, and Andrew with his black glossy hair and leather clothes did, indeed, epitomize the image of rock 'n' roll. Andrew would have loved being a rock star. He fantasized about seeing big blowup photos of his hollow self, say, on a Times Square billboard, and that sent him into a self-absorbed ecstasy. However, Andrew lacked musicality. His song writing was weak. Vocals, guitar and piano playing, and stage presence, too, were also lacking.

Then there were his guitars. Stacked in their cases, they reached the ceiling of the tiny closet-sized apartment. It didn't matter how many guitars he had, guitars piled as high up as the Empire State Building, he still needed to learn to play *one* and write a good song, and then think of image—how he looked playing the thing—but that was not his way.

He wasn't a great hairdresser either, but he did manage to hold a job at a very trendy place where he met the latest and greatest, like the character in *Shampoo*. Andrew loved The Beatles and cried the cold December night of John

Lennon's assassination. My boss lived in the building behind the Dakota and heard the shots. "It sounded like firecrackers," he said.

My boss was uneasy with Andrew, and my friends from work didn't like him either, except David, who was curious about a particular part of Andrew's anatomy. Leave it to David, he once came to work late, buttoning his pants and said, "Sorry about that. I was having sex with the garbage man." David smoked pot before work, at lunchtime, and after work. We got along well and had fun together, but he could get edgy and occasionally blow up at the clients. Once, exasperated, he slammed his hands on the counter so hard, it shook, and the client jumped back. He could be a charmer, though, and conducted an affair with a much older woman who owned a chain of sporting-goods stores. She was loud and abrasive but endowed him with gifts and lent him a financial hand. Ambitious, energetic David ran in many directions. He freelanced for the elderly wife of a very, very famous songwriter and babysat for the shop's owners. He was inquisitive. "How does Andrew get into those leather pants?" he marveled.

He just pulled them on, of course, without underpants, and pulled them off. They were the most-known, most-worn leather pants on the island of Manhattan, and probably the Bronx and Staten Island, too. Andrew with the roaming pants was known in Queens and Brooklyn and wherever else in the world the roué might be tempted.

In photos of Andrew, he stands apart from the group. My

sisters didn't like him, and neither did my father. Curiously, the only one who liked him a little was my mother. She thought he looked like Tyrone Power. The only thing I liked about Andrew was his mother. Her husband, Andrew's father, was an extremely handsome man similar to Paul Newman but taller and better looking. He turned out to be a good-for-nothing, drinking bum and left the family. His ex-wife supported her three children and elderly parents by working as a waitress on Staten Island. She was a simple, kind woman. We visited her on Monday evenings. She picked us up at the ferry terminal, drove us to her house, and served a big spaghetti dinner with crabs or steak and, for dessert, bought cannoli. I ate so much, she asked Andrew if I didn't eat the rest of the week.

Andrew worked in the trendy shop with Ruth, a woman we all liked about as much as we liked him. She was just as vain but not as handsome. Ruth sprawled spread-eagle in her hairdresser's chair wearing a tiny kilt and bootlings, straightening her long hair with a giant brush and blow dryer, all day between clients. She had several claims to fame. The first, her sister lived with a dinosaur rock star in Westchester. The rock star, Frampton somebody, had bought the sister a Datsun sports car for her birthday. We asked, "A Datsun? From a rich rock star?" The second of Ruth's claims was that she had once cut Mick Jagger's hair while wearing a short skirt and no underpants, hoping Mick might catch a glance. Surely, Mick must have had better things to look at. And third, Ruth knew a carpenter who had worked on John and Yoko's kitchen, and she had tagged along. We fully relished *la pointe de la sauce* (the spicing of the sauce) of the Ruth stories and spent hours telling and re-telling bits and pieces of them to each other.

Francois owned the Prince Street shop where Andrew and Ruth worked and lugubriously lounged and gossiped. Ruth and Francois had once been an item and lived together, but he'd taken off to Rivington Street with a very nice boyfriend. Francois invited us to dine. I thought he might cook a beautiful French meal, but we ate rice and beans and perched on plastic milk cartons. A baby rat ran across the room, tiny feet scrabbling against the hard floor. No one said anything, and I kept my scream to myself so as not to embarrass my host. That was one of the last times I saw Francois—a large, loud, opinionated, wild Charles De Gaulle downtown French man with a monumental Gallic nose.

Rivington Street, and those narrow, crowded, dark streets in lower Manhattan, were the last frontier, the last place downtown where rents were cheap. Francois and his friend paid about $250 a month rent in the early '80s for their sizeable digs. However, the area came with a price. Jill had a friend who lived there, too, and said that the first time you came home and found a dead body lying across your doorstep, you thought you were cool and living on the edge, the wild west, wild east. The second time it happened, it became a drag.

(Incidentally, again, in *The Doors*, the place where Jim engages in the Celtic handfasting ceremony looks much like an apartment at the historic LaGrange Terrace on Lafayette Street, near Astor Place, where a friend of a friend lived. A big, strapping person, she engaged in brutal fistfights with her landlord. The rent was cheap then, and he tried to physically force her out, and he threw her down the stairs. Cheap rent often came with a stiff price.)

One time, Ruth cut Billy Idol's hair. Jill and Daniel peeked into the shop to have a look. Blond Billy sat idle while Ruth danced around and did her thing. Apparently, Ruth was getting old or hadn't had the time to remove her undies. Billy looked blasé. Ruth reluctantly gave up and went back to her lunch of cold string beans that she ate with her fingers.

Later, she would enter Cocaine Anonymous.

The sister may still be with the rock star. Ms. Silver from the Bronx wasn't about to give up her pot of gold and, maybe, a better car.

Ruth, Francois, Andrew, Daniel, Jill, and I worked a Betsey Johnson fashion show. I did makeup, but my interest in the downtown circus was at a new low. No one got along backstage— bickering, backstabbing, the usual. It was crowded, noisy, and hot, and I was bored and tired. Joan Jett gave me the eye, a big salacious eye. Oh, great, I thought. I should have directed her toward hot-pants Andrew, they could have worked something out, but I went home instead.

One of my last dates with Andrew was going to the Grammy Awards at Radio City Music Hall. Some publicist had given him tickets, and he was probably up to his usual tricks with her. It wasn't a terribly exciting event; the Bee Gees won. They were standing in the lobby as we left.

As our relationship dwindled down, my style changed more and more. I wore a gray cashmere sweater and straight navy wool skirt; my makeup was minimal. Andrew arrived dressed, as always, like a rock star in black leather jeans and jacket. His face fell when he saw me. "Aren't you going to change?" he asked bewildered. No. I wasn't. I no longer cared to be among the hip. He was going to get tickets for an upcoming Marvin Gaye concert, also at Radio City. I wanted to go, but not with him. I didn't go. "Sexual Healing" was Andrew's favorite song: small wonder.

Eventually, the fighting with Andrew got way out of hand. We were like two dogs destined to never get along. I didn't like or trust him. I couldn't believe a word he said, and he was a poor liar.

When push came to shove, naturally, I shoved back. How did push come to shove? Well, Andrew had lost the lease on his Fifth Avenue apartment. I don't know how. Maybe it'd never actually been his; he had lived there with a girl before I met him, but she'd moved to Florida and soon married some-one else. Basically, he'd had no place to go but to his mother's in Staten Island. It would have been better if he'd gone there, but I in my stupidity temporarily allowed him to stay at the tiny East Fifth Street apartment. He brought two cats that also had nowhere to go. He didn't like the cats, and the cats didn't like him. I didn't know anything about cats, but they made me itch and made my nose stuffy, my throat tightened, and my eyes swelled. The cats seemed to like me, though, and liked to sleep on my head or crawl across my chest when I tried to sleep. I couldn't sleep with cats purring on me and my head.

It wasn't the cats that brought on the incident, but in a way, they didn't help. Andrew lied a big stupid lie, once too many times. He had been out the whole night. Where was he after work? Was he in harm's way? Was he dead in the street? What should I do? He didn't get back until I was getting dressed for work in the morning.

"Where were you all night?" I asked, concerned. He looked disheveled and worn from too much drink.

"Out playing cards," he replied.

He didn't play cards. Why hadn't he called? He was with a girl. I knew those slimy leather pants.

"Stop telling stories. You and your cats are going to have to pack up and go back to your card game, because you're not staying here."

One thing led to another, voices escalated, tensions rose, words became more heated, and then it happened. Andrew hit me in the nose, and I felt the blood. I let loose and went bloody nuts. "*Out! Now!* Go and take those *cats!*" The poor cats were hiding, nowhere to be seen.

Andrew fled the building and into the strong arms of those wonderful New York City police from the Ninth Precinct, who just so happened to be leaving their shift. They grabbed him as he ran onto the street and brought him back to my door. I met massive Officer McKenna.

"What's the trouble, ma'am?" They looked at me with

the blood running from my nose.

"That idiot *hit* me!" I yelled. "Take him away!"

"We'll take care of him, but first let's get you an ambulance," the cops offered.

An ambulance? Oh, boy!

What happened? It was a blur. I went to the Ninth to fill out papers. I went to the hospital emergency room and called Jean to tell her I wouldn't be in work that Saturday morning. It was probably the first time I'd ever called in sick. Later, when I told her why, she hated Andrew and wanted to harm him. Andrew spent the day and night in jail; his poor, humble mother had to bail the moron out, and I was sorry for that. It must have been quite an experience for him in The Tombs. I wondered how the inmates liked having Mr. Jailhouse Rock among them.

Weeks later, I visited Andrew's sweet Sicilian grandfather. "Glad to see you kids put down the boxing gloves," he said kindly. I felt bad that the nice old fella knew. I didn't see him again until he died, when Andrew brought a new girlfriend, an exotic dancer, to the funeral. She was dressed in a tight suede fringed jacket and a lot of makeup. I went with my fascinated mother, who thought the girl was something else. I didn't care, and that was a great feeling. Andrew was past.

After the emergency room doctor repaired me that day, Francois, of the great big Gallic nose, knew an esteemed Fifth Avenue plastic surgeon he was eager for me to see. "He ez very Wasp doctor. Heez work very refined. The office ez decorated in wood paneling and equestrian preents. You must go to heam. No one else, just heam. He ez an *artiste*."

Well, the elegant Wasp plastic surgeon said, "Yes, we must fix your nose properly," and I was sent to the world-class Manhattan Eye, Ear, Nose, and Throat Hospital, where all the socialites went for their noses and nips and tucks. I was given doses of drugs and, etherized upon the table, went sleepily into the nether world. So this is how Johnny Thunders feels, I said to myself as I slipped under. So this is Long Bill Bull Lee when he's feeling good. "Count from ten backwards," the anesthesiologist instructed me. Euphorically, I mumbled "ten," slid into my drug-induced haze and woke up once to hear the file on my nose, but it didn't hurt, not one little bit. I imagined myself as Bernini's *St. Teresa in Ecstasy*, levitating out of this realm with that blissful look on my face, naked feet free from the sheet and limp hands dangling from my sides, *to sleep, to sleep, perchance to dream...* I, like William Butler Yeats, being poor, had only my dreams.

It did hurt when I came to and my nose was stuffed with gauze packing for several days. I shared my hospital stay with an elderly socialite who, after her facelift, looked very much like Mickey Rourke after his last fight. Caked blood had dried on her swollen face. "No, darling, it doesn't hurt *a-tall*," she said, eyes black. It looked like it hurt. It looked like it hurt a lot.

At the hospital, Dr. Gian Franco Rossini, a Harvard-educated plastic surgeon who, with Dr. Wasp, fixed my nose, took a liking to me, and then took me out to fancy restaurants in his big navy Mercedes Benz with the slippery leather seats.

Sometimes he cooked for me. Gian Franco was short, pudgy, and ill dressed, not at all handsome. He thought nothing of wearing a plaid jacket with striped pants and mismatched tie, strange for a Northern Italian from Milano. "If I could," he said, "I'd wear a bikini to work." It was a good thing he couldn't, because it would have been unseemly. We had little in common, good old Gian Franco and I, but he was pleasant, and the aperitifs and fancy dinners and his car were fine. I liked his Park Avenue apartment, too, but wasn't sure I would have him as part of the package.

Gian Franco took two Italian friends and me out to dinner one brisk Sunday afternoon. He wasn't ashamed to pick me up at my modest Fifth Street abode with his fellow Park Avenues in that deluxe automobile. I, however, felt the shabbiness of my street acutely as I stepped from the worn, dirty curb into the golden coach and we drove to Long Island. They were all about twenty years older than I, and one of them was a famous Italian journalist, Sylvia someone who spoke in melodious Italian and English and waved her expressive hands and arms. Once I sank into the scrumptious, soft beige seat, listening to her aria, they could have taken me to the moon. The day sparkled, and we stopped at the beach. I wore a pair of expensive Jackie O-type alligator shoes that pinched as we walked. Still, it felt refreshing to be out in the sun and by the ocean on that cool, clear spring day. Then we indulged in a late-day Italian seafood fest with lots of nice wine, and everyone talked and talked and laughed an Italian laugh, and I sat there smiling at the halcyon day.

As for Andrew, he was done. Andrew's mother gave the cats a home. As for Paul McCartney, well, he hasn't been happening since Hamburg. Francois was eager to see my nose, and then he had that great Gallic De Gaullian nose of his reduced by the wonderful Dr. Wasp. Francois looked quite handsome with his newly sized proboscis, but then, soon after, sadly, a gunman in the subway killed him in a random act. The world was a little less French with Francois gone, downtown more grim. As for me, I had had enough and retired in my early twenties from a wonderful job, left my beloved apartment and friends, and enrolled in a Catholic all-women's college taught by the Sisters of Mercy at a convent surrounded by a high wall. On the other side was a large Hasidic community. There was absolutely nothing to do at school except study, and that is what I did.

It was our parents who instilled in us our love of New York City. Our parents took us to the city for outings as children, then when we were young teenagers, they drove us in, but gave us the freedom of a couple of hours of our own time to explore the wonderful city. It was easier to park downtown, so on late Sunday mornings and early afternoons we headed downtown, to Washington Square, Chinatown, and Little Italy. We loved that, roaming around on our own, hoping passersby thought we were real New Yorkers. Jill and I hopped out of the car—hoping no one noticed we were with Mom and Dad, but that's how kids think—and we would all meet back at the car at a specified time. We were always faithful to our obligation to be there punctually to comply with our parents and, again, hope no one noticed we were with them as we dove into the car and headed back to New Jersey.

Jill and I walked around, looked in the shops, bought shoes, and watched the people and street performers if they weren't too loud and obvious. We glanced at boys, and they might look at us, but it was too early in the day to run into any Joey Clams or Frankie Boneses. We had little adventures, bought ice cream cones or lemon ices, and checked out the health food stores and pastry shops. On Mulberry and Mott Streets we stopped to look at curious storefront "social clubs." The Sons of Tripoli Social Club? What was that? This was in the days when a few old Italian people still lived on mean streets in those interesting neighborhoods. There might be a scattering of elderly Italian gents hanging around, sitting outside, a few straddling backwards old wooden chairs. We peeked in the window if no one was outside but couldn't see much, a dark mostly empty room, a few tables, a little bar, an espresso machine. "Well, Jill, let's go in and have a soda." Show-off me, like Shackelton I lead the way.

An ancient man emerged from behind the dusty counter. "What you want?"

His manner wasn't particularly welcoming. The day was hot.

"Soda?"

He slowly reached for two tiny glasses, carefully opened the small bottles with a bottle opener, poured the soda in the glasses, and charged us two dollars. We drank the warm ginger ale, said thank you, and left. It looked as if we were the first customers in years. That was our social club experience. Of course, we discussed it between ourselves, quietly, and wondered what it was about. I didn't understand the significance of the club until after seeing *The Pope of Greenwich Village*.

After the draining ten rounds with Andrew, a new tenant appeared in my building. Matthew Bertolli's loft on North Moore Street had had a fire, and he was temporarily staying at East Fifth Street. A powerfully built man and a straight shooter, he presented a different image than the other pale, skinny boys I knew. He dressed in work clothes and steel-toed shoes and looked as if he knew how to do practical things like fix machines and build houses.

He learned of the incident with Andrew.

"You wanna have his legs broken?"

I weighed the issue and said, "No. That's over. He's not worth it."

Matthew kept two Dobermans that he trained to guard the loft, but he seemed lonely. He had recently broken up with a Maria Ruiz, who must have been one spicy spitfire. Vincent Gallo had an interest in her, too. Apparently, Maria and I resembled each other, but our paths never crossed, and that was probably a good thing. Matthew's relationship with her sounded explosive, and I had had enough fireworks of my own. We became friends. He worked as a master cabinet-maker and spent a lot of time doing custom work for yacht owners. He had been married to a woman from Newark, New Jersey, whose father was a mob big shot, so he said. They had a child, but it didn't seem like he spent time with his daughter.

Matthew had grown up on King Street, near the Holland Tunnel, when it was still a poor Italian neighborhood. I felt safe and protected with Matthew as my friend. He was generous and did carpentry work in my apartment and crafted a cabinet for me from white ash. When Kooperberg, the landlord, saw it, he was duly impressed and asked if I was an interior designer. Kooperberg became a lot nicer after that and offered to provide a reference if need be.

Matthew drank strong red wine from a small juice glass and smoked cigars. Being a good Italian, he took care to feed me. He cooked and brought food down or, once in a while, treated me to dinner at Raoul's bistro on Prince Street. Andrew lived four or five blocks east. When I was sick, Matthew bought me chicken soup from the Second Avenue Deli.

Matthew injured his hand at work and had to take time off. To compensate for lost income, he took a job as a driver for an exclusive Upper East Side florist. My tiny apartment was soon filled with exotic flowers. Ironically, just when it was so beautiful, I was about to leave it, but photos remain of orchids, tulips, and some unidentifiable blossoms. Roses. Lilacs, hyacinth, violets—the studio was as fragrant as the flower-filled home of *Madama Butterfly*. Being coddled by two nurturing Italians was balm. Life was good again, and I was in the food. Neither thought my moving back to New

Jersey was a smart idea. I had doubts, too, and became so anxious that, at night, it felt as if the bed spun.

Just when I thought Andrew was about gone, he called my mother and told her I was dating a mafioso. Andrew! How dare he? He who had turned my hair to mash! He who didn't change his clothes! The great liar with the sliding pants and nothing in his head and the old black banana tree and the girls dashing out of his apartment like a scene from *Le Nozze di Figaro* with playmates hiding behind doors, under sheets, beneath beds, and jumping from windows to escape confrontation, except this was New York City and jumping from windows wasn't practical.

Why should he have called my mother? I was livid, enraged, but first I had to calm my mother, no easy task. "No, Mom. Matthew is a friend who helped me to do some work. He's not my boyfriend. Andrew is angry because I won't see him, and his imagination is running wild." To tell my mother about the incident was unthinkable. It wasn't the time to tell her Matthew had proposed my being part of a gold-smuggling operation either. "Here's a way to make some real money," he said. No. That's not for me. Life in a South American jail didn't seem agreeable. Again, I had had enough.

Andrew called. "Who was the plastic surgeon who fixed your nose? Mine has a bump I don't like, and I'm going to have it fixed, too." The conceited, thoughtless dog—poor Francois in the grave with his new nose, and the blackguard Andrew thinking only of his looks and foolish self. I slammed the phone down.

Hardened hearts of stone, false world! Get me to a nunnery.

Back in sad lost New Jersey, I took instructions at a driving school with a gentle elderly man. It didn't take me long, and learning to drive was a big accomplishment. Jill and my mother never learned. I bought a little car to use in college and after. Every year driving became easier until it became harder: more traffic, longer commutes, crazier drivers, bad road conditions, and, later, SUVs that blocked visibility. But no matter how bad the New Jersey commute, it was like a vacation compared to commuting to New York. Commuting to the city, I got up early, dressed in good clothes, and then took the trip in either by bus or train. Traveling on mass transit, I always felt dirty and in need of another shower and change of clothes when I got to my destination.

Then, there were the other commuters. Most were tired like me, but there would be the occasional chatterbox or madwoman that would rant the whole ugly trip on the turnpike and through the tunnel. To find a seat on the train was sheer luck. By the time I got home at night, I wanted to burn my clothes and scrub my skin. Then the whole thing would start again, first thing in the morning. It just wasn't worth it. My car, however, was clean. I set the climate control and had the luxury of bringing things I needed during the day, without considering how to carry them: extra shoes, a sweater, books, and food. Comfort came with me where I needed to go. To listen to a tape while driving was a treat.

My greatest fear in New Jersey, on the other hand, was driving with and against raging motor vehicles and being killed in a highway crash.

During the East Fifth days, I walked the few dingy blocks from home, past the heavy closed doors of Cooper Union—a place I never once entered—and then climbed down the dirty steps holding on to the clammy metal handrail to the frantic Astor Place Station subway platform. It wasn't a long ride to West Fifty-fifth Street, maybe twenty-five minutes, but I always felt anxious and grimy, and looked over my shoulder. It was a relief when the train came, and a bigger relief to get off the usually filthy subway and climb the stairs up and out onto the street. Most of all, I detested the dank air, damp smell, the odor of stale urine, but I didn't like the crowds, dirt, or noise either. From the height of the platform, I watched out for the rats darting under the train tracks. My greatest fears in New York were getting raped or killed, encounters with rats or bugs, and unpleasantness in the mad subways. Once in a while, weather permitting, I walked the fifty blocks north and the blocks east to west, and that was downright enjoyable, seeing the city on foot, admiring the architecture and shop windows and *le dernier cri* (the latest thing) and street fashions.

The fashion wears out more apparel than the man.

—Much Ado about Nothing

8

REFLECTIONS ON EAST FIFTH STREET

AND ODE TO GINSBERG

∽

ONCE IN A WHILE, my apartment was a refuge for my brother. Keven and I had never been close, though we were less than a year apart. Was he born with pure unbridled temperament—incapable of anything but complete, vociferous honesty—or was it something more? My brother is as dark and quiet as Heathcliff, but when he becomes frustrated, he's volatile. To have a relationship with him was impossible, so even though he had sisters, his best friends were dogs, strays he would find on the street or at the shelter: Rocky, Lucky, and Scruffy came into his life one after the other. They were cute little puppies devoted to their owner. He took them with him walking on long, long, walks. From East Fifth Street, he walked to the Bronx or to Brooklyn. What he did there remains a mystery; maybe he went to a park or zoo, had something to eat, or shopped, but he liked the old ethnic neighborhoods and felt at home there. Along the way he and his dog meet acquaintances. "Hi, Rocky! How ya doing, boy?"

Rocky was a gray mixed poodle, shaggy and snippy. Scruffy a friendly, white-mixed terrier, remained my favorite; and then there was Lucky, perhaps the dog least mannered and most out of control. He stood a small, lean mixed shepherd with distinctive markings and sharp teeth. Well into old age, he was mistaken for a pup, because he was so physically fit. Keven wasn't communicative, so we often said if Lucky could talk he'd have stories to tell.

Lucky habitually snatched food that didn't belong to him and nipped people. He sprang up on all fours on my mother's dining room table like a flying kangaroo to help himself to a cake, or he stuck his head under the broiler to quickly extract a chicken. Until the end of his long life, he stayed sly and sneaky and lightning fast. Lucky was fond of pizza and made it his specialty to grab slices from unsuspecting passers-by on busy New York City streets. Up he jumped and helped himself to a snack. Lucky and I got along just okay. Occasionally, he grabbed my wrist in his mouth, but I usually had treats to soothe him. I talked softly and asked him to behave. We played, as best as I could with a temperamental, rude dog, who was interested in just one thing, food, but I never attempted to remove anything from his grip. He exposed sharp fangs and let out a low menacing warning, and I knew better. He looked dead serious. Still, Lucky was welcomed because he protected Keven on their urban sojourns.

Either on a Friday or Saturday night, Keven might come

and sleep under the loft, he and his dog. He had a key, so he could come and go as he pleased. They got up early in the morning, as soon as it was light, and off they went to explore the New York City boroughs. That was one of the few things I could share with him. He enjoyed it, and I was happy to know he was safe, so it saddened my heart that I would be unable to give him that little comfort.

Later, he would marry, and he and his sweet, simple, innocent wife would have two boys, both children with autism. (Keven seemed to be the bearer of an Ethan Frome-type struggle.) That was my informal introduction to autism, a heartbreakingly cruel neurological disorder that impairs communication, behavior, and social skills. It would take two more decades before coming face to face with the sobering reality of working with children with autism.

(After marrying, for the first time in my life, I moved to the leafy but dull suburbs. The days on East Fifth Street were long in the past, and I couldn't find a job. After fingerprints and stacks of forms, I became a substitute teacher. The pay was eighty dollars per diem, what Cher paid in 1982 to have her eyebrows shaped in twenty minutes. Work as a substitute paraprofessional was available every day, but the pay was only ten dollars an hour, the price of a good-quality lipstick twenty years before.

A school paraprofessional works as an aide in the classroom with special-needs children. They may be children with autism or Down syndrome, or confined to a wheel chair. Some special- education classes may only have eight children with a teacher and a paraprofessional for each student. All this was new to me, difficult, and wrenching. It opened my eyes to another world: a world of almost silent screams and loud piercing screams, a world of frustrations, frustration after frustration all day, a world of trips to the bathrooms and bathroom accidents, a world of helplessness and little hope and pleading broken hearts and what seemed to be desperate, unheard, unanswered prayers. Sometimes, I had to turn my head from the child to hide tears or turn to the wall and wipe my streaming face.

The women who work as paraprofessionals with children with the greatest needs spend a good part of the day taking children to the toilet and changing diapers. Assisting a child in a wheelchair to the toilet takes a long time and may involve the help of more than one person. It might involve a special harness and a great deal of care. It's a struggle. I was a complete novice at this undertaking, but my eyes were left wide open after working as a substitute paraprofessional for four school terms.

I applied for a full-time position but didn't get the job. Overwhelmed by emotion, I cried at the interview, as my boss on West Fifty-fifth Street had feared long ago. There were so many to weep for: the picture-perfect princess with the blonde curls who had almost no verbal skills, the young women who needed the bathroom harness and two aides to help, the handsome little boy who looked like Jesus de Jesus but couldn't differentiate colors, an immaculately groomed brother and sister, both children with autism; and I wept for my brother and his family. I sat there and sobbed, could not compose myself, and the interviewer handed me a tissue.)

When it was my turn to leave home and move to New York, it was less intense than Kris's experience, but it was still marked by some of my mother's drama. For one thing, I was less prized. I wasn't considered brilliant. I was considered scatterbrained. How many times had my mother asked me to take out the freshly baked bread from the oven, and I'd just plumb forgotten? Many had been the times, too late, I'd smelled the smell of the burned black crust. My high school photo was unflattering. My untamed black hair covered much of my face, and I looked more like Yoko Ono, whom I liked, than Elizabeth Taylor. My hair drove my mother crazy. "You have such a pretty face, but you hide it with that hair! Get that hair away from your face!" She got so angry. At that time, it was hard to find a magazine cover girl who wasn't a blue-eyed blonde. Yoko and I had a few things in common: our black hair and dark eyes; she was an artist and I wanted to be one; and we both liked John and New York. Secondly, Mills the dangerous predator had soiled me, and third, I had shown little promise in high school, and my painting didn't count. However, my mother did cry and told me I wouldn't be able to pay my New York rent. She also called my home on East Fifth Street a tenement. "Why do you want to move to a neighborhood like that?" she asked, perplexed with images of reeking turn-of-the-century tenements and squalor in her imagination. I needed to live in New York, and it was all

I could afford; that's why.

I worked nonstop to pay my rent and saved a small sum for the future: Perhaps I could finish buying an education. My parents were smart, practical people and had shown me how to save. As for my apartment being a tenement, it wasn't that bad. True, it was small, but I wasn't that big, had few possessions, and lived there alone. Jean had given me an antique dressing table with a mirror, and I had a white wicker loveseat with red silk pillows, two wooden chairs, a mattress, and a ficus tree. That was it, no television. The place had two large south-facing windows, so there was good light and a pleasant view of the stately townhouses on the other side of the shady, tree-lined street.

The apartment had been newly renovated: new sheet rock, exposed brick, new flooring. I paid eight times in rent what the Puerto Rican man next door paid. Within a short period of time, my pot-smoking-on-the-fire-escape neighbor was evicted, his apartment renovated, and the new neighbor paid more than I did. All the tenants were young working people I didn't know well. A fair-skinned, blue-eyed, turbaned individual used the fire escape as a staircase. He climbed up carrying take-out food, once in a while, and waved at me through the window. A journalist who worked in Washington, D.C., had an apartment in the building and used it when he was in New York, but he, too, paid enviably low rent and was forced out. The journalist was more vocal about his eviction than my neighbor, to no avail.

Because the police station was on the next block, McSorley's Ale House two blocks away, and what had once been the Fillmore East, now a gay disco called The Saint, was just around the corner, the area was noisy, especially on weekend nights with partying tourists and patrol cars racing to emergencies, light and sirens activated. Often enough, someone would tear down the street after a late night out, overturning every garbage can on the sidewalk, making a racket, and waking up the whole neighborhood and every dog in it. Residents flung open their windows and soundly curse the rascal in the early morning air. "What the hell, what the *hell*," someone screamed from a window. "What's going *on* down there?"

The East Village—called the counter-culture capitol of the world—was popular with young people and artists and radicals, and living there had its own amusing rewards. You never knew who or what you might run into on the street. It could be members of the band you'd seen at a club the night before, or it might be Lou Reed. The poet Allen Ginsberg lived in the neighborhood and was frequently spotted walking about. Ginsberg was the best known of the Beat poets. "Hey," someone on the street howled at him—probably a tourist— "the beat goes on, man!" At the time, "the sorrowful poetic conman with the dark mind that is Carlo Marx," as described by Jack Kerouac, was in his mid-fifties, small, and gray. He was still, of course, a horn-rimmed, weak-eyed intellectual with a kind sad heart but not quite Alvah Goldbook the young hepcat with wild black hair. Like Groucho Marx, he was always rushing and very thin; maybe he couldn't afford food, living the life of a poet. As Ginsberg the bard wailed, "When can I go into the supermarket and buy what I need with my good looks?" No wives in the avocados or babies in the tomatoes, on line at the grocery, someone of approachable note might stand behind me, and perhaps I'd meet a new acquaintance or be invited to a party or gallery event or happening. The streets of the East Village were an extension of the clubs—a village within a village—and the members were clad in their black uniforms with youth as their shining badge.

There were always crowds: lines in the small supermarket—where Walt Whitman (so adored by the irrepressible Roberto, Bob, in *Down by Law*) eyed the grocery boys, lines at the bank, laundry mat, and deli, but the teeming tenement life of struggling mostly Eastern European Jewish families with multitudes of children of almost a century past—when the Gershwin brothers lived on Second Avenue—was long gone, even though that is the lower East Side, where my mother had it in her head that I dwelled. A few remnants of that period existed, and the buildings remained.

The owner of the Second Avenue Deli would be on line at the bank with a huge wad of cash in one pants pocket and a gun in the other. (Years later, he would be killed during a hold- up, and that case remains unsolved.) Once in a while, Jill and I would get a pastrami sandwich at the famous Jewish deli. It was clean, tidy, safe, and usually mobbed, but we didn't mind. Smells of pastrami and corned beef filled the space. Display cases contained interesting things like *kasha varniskes*, and we wondered what they were. Jars of yellow deli mustard and bowls of cabbage and carrot health salad sat on the tables. The cabbage salad tasted like old people's food. Early Sunday morning was probably the only quiet time in the streets.

It occurred to me that the happiest people, the friendliest people, and the most sincere people in Manhattan were the dogs. Whenever I needed to find a friendly face, I'd meet a loyal doggie, tied up outside the grocery store or deli, and he'd provide a cheerful look, warm eyes, a wagging tail, or fall into the play position. He wasn't concerned with fashion or style or being rich or famous or chic; his only want was a tasty snack or the company of a friend.

The neighborhood was just starting to gentrify, so there was still plenty of funky stuff to provide character and characters, but I lived without incident, with the exception of the incident with Andrew.

Along Second Avenue, starting at St. Mark's Church in-the-Bowery—long ago in 1651 "The Bowery" had been Governor of New Amsterdam Peter Stuyvesant's farm (*bouweries* means farm in Dutch)—the neighborhood got interesting going south. On the corner of St. Mark's Place and Second was Gem Spa Magazines, the birthplace of the egg cream and a place where The New York Dolls posed for an album cover. With regret, I must admit, I never downed a famed egg cream. I didn't know what an egg cream was and didn't like eggs—an egg cream has no eggs but is made of syrup, soda, and milk—so I didn't indulge. Also, I thought the place might be dirty and was afraid to go in there. Jill felt the same way. Other old-time places of interest that I hesitated to patronize were the B&H Dairy, Kiev, Moishe's Bake Shop, and Binibon. I shouldn't have been so squeamish about the old and worn, and now, seeing how the world has become so homogenized with bland, giant chain stores, I regret vanished New York.

The Binibon was an unpretentious, busy all-night eatery on the corner of my very own block, Second Avenue and Fifth Street. A notorious late night, early morning literary murder took place there in 1981. The morning after the fatal stabbing, the author and killer received a favorable review in the Sunday *New York Times*. The reviewer gave thanks to the murderer's mentor, Norman Mailer, for his help in getting the book published and for his role in getting the convict out on parole six weeks before. The victim, a waiter, was also a writer, a playwright. My parents visited me that Sunday afternoon. By then, all the excitement had ceased, but the yellow crime scene tape blocked off the corner and waved at my parents with all their fears and concerns.

Years after leaving the East Village, there was an unusually gruesome murder. The deranged murderer had killed a young Martha Graham student and dancer who had been living in his apartment for the previous sixteen days. The young Swiss woman was desperate for a place to stay, so she unknowingly moved in with an insane man. After he killed her, he allegedly cooked her remains and distributed the soup to the homeless in Tompkins Square Park. More than ten years before that murder, Tompkins Square Park was a little too on the edge for me. I went there once with Daniel on a warm summer day but didn't feel safe. Summertime, the living is easy, and people lived on the streets. Whole sets of living room furniture occupied a vacant lot, and people cooked food on an open fire. It was an apartment without walls. Speakers blared music into the air, and babies cried. I returned to the limited comforts of the East Fifth Street lair startled and secure behind closed bourgeois doors.

I seldom ventured into the southern East Village—the lower East Side—onto what I called the name streets: Chrystie, Forsyth, Eldridge, Allen, Orchard, Ludlow, Essex, Norfolk, Suffolk, Clinton, Pitt. I was just too scared, although fascinated. I had heard too many stories of junkies and rats, and I could just feel them crawling out of their holes, waiting to pounce on me. There was a restaurant on the corner of Rivington and Chrystie that captured my imagination, though I may have past it only once or twice: Sammy's Rumanian Steak House. What was it? Did gypsies dance in the basement? Did Mayor Koch eat there? I hadn't a clue. Of course, I never went there, but over the years I read about it—enormous portions of food, chicken fat, and frozen vodka, an old-time Jewish restaurant that hadn't bothered to spruce up.

Speaking of McSorley's, Kris knew the owner of that fine old tavern, established in 1854. Ritchie was a former New York City detective. On a cold March 17, Kris, Jill, and I attended the glorious St. Patrick's Day parade on Fifth Avenue. The bagpipes and horses, and the endless rows of navy uniforms and marching bands, were without rival. It started to snow, and the wind picked up, so we moved on down to East Seventh Street. A long line twisted outside the historic pub, and we took our place. "Perth Amboy!" we heard someone shout. Ritchie motioned toward us. "Perth Amboy to the front of the line, if you please!" That was our summons. We smiled at each other, giggled, and went inside to the smell of old, ale-soaked wood. McSorley's held fast as a mostly male club in those days, so everyone was happy to see three lovely young ladies. We got our mugs from the rubber-aproned, Wellington-booted bartender, who managed to carry two cold ones per finger. McSorley's small menu listed ham sandwiches or cheese on a plate. That was it, the menu. The plates came with rings of raw onions that we hung on our ears. Behold, the hottest mustard on earth. Held at arm's length, the fumes brought tears to my eyes. We weren't there for the food; we were there for the camaraderie.

Before you knew it, jolly frat boys hoisted me on top of one of the round wooden tables. It felt good to be up there, on top of the world. My shiny green pants had been altered to fit. "Hip, hip, hooray! Hip, hip, hooray for Green Pants!" shouted the lads. We laughed and yelled to each other on top of the noisy, rollicking crowd. If Mom could see me now, I thought. We had a blast. Weeks later, my voice remained sore, but it was worth it. The green pants had split and were in the trash.

My sister Jackie didn't care for New York, so she came just once to East Fifth with her friends. The apartment was so small that they had to stand outside on the fire escape to all fit, and the fire escape wasn't that big or sturdy either. Of the four girls in our family, Jackie was the obedient, dutiful daughter who most listened to our parents. She liked sailing and sports and boys who liked sports, so we didn't do much together in those days. Jackie was never a hippie, and in high school she was so filled with team spirit that most of her clothes were red and white, the school's colors. Cheerful and outgoing, with beautiful, dark, expressive eyes, Jackie had a slim athletic frame and ran the entire 26.2 miles of the New York City Marathon.

Her friend worked himself up from stock boy to an executive at Gem Records. He generously provided us with all the latest imports from England, boxes and boxes of albums, singles, and promotional materials. The Clash ranked the best. No one I knew liked the Sex Pistols, but the Gem Record exec had given us Sex Pistol T-shirts, and we wore them. We were the first kids on the block, the first in the tri-state area, to acquire such dubious treasures. A photo of Jill in Spain, posed against a blue sky and black movie poster, shows her clad in a Sex Pistols T-shirt.

Sid Vicious, and his girlfriend Nancy, stumbled out of Max's one bitter night. He was very pale, very thin, very young, and very wasted. Sid Vicious was the whitest man I ever saw, white as a death shroud. He was a kid, a white lost lamb, gone, stumbling like an angry lost soul against the freezing black city. She, too, appeared gone, but stronger than he; she seemed to support him, two lost souls against time in their black leather jackets. Nancy tripped behind him and into a cab as Jill and I looked on with feigned nonchalance, but that was one of the saddest sights I ever saw. With the slam of the cab door, the yellow taxi tore down deserted Park Avenue South into the icy darkness and grim rock 'n' roll history.

The record executive had an extra ticket, so I went with him to see Harry Chapin at a theater in New Brunswick. I wasn't expecting to like so tame a performer, but Harry was great, and it was a memorable show.

Daniel had been cooking at my apartment. I came home, and he greeted me with a strange expression on his face. "There are bugs in the stove." We looked at each other in horror and knew what kind of bugs they were, the disgusting kind that have rent-free reign in New York. Daniel was still living with his parents in a comfortable, spotless, suburban house. I had been raised in a spotless home, too, so we were duly repulsed. The bugs represented filth, slovenliness, poverty, and tenement living. My mother had warned me.

That was it. Daniel helped me, and we tore the stove apart and cleaned it with hot soapy water. We scrubbed every surface and threw away whatever little food we had. Then, I rushed to the pharmacy, bought big jars of boric acid, and filled every visible crack and crevice with the white powder. The apartment had always been clean, but now it was sterilized. Those sanitary high standards were the norm, and visitors were always amazed at how immaculate the apartment was.

People took me out to eat more often than I cooked, but I tired of eating in restaurants. During the Andrew days, he took me out almost every night—with money filched from the cash register at work (this was before the advent of ubiquitous security cameras and computerized registers)—usually to 102 Second Avenue, a new, bright, and spacious white-walled and young people's restaurant with polished wood floors. A giant clock with large hands was mounted on the wall. Locals filled the tables, and hip music played as loudly as it played in the clubs, so you couldn't hear what the person next to you was saying, making it perfect for us. Once a week, we ate at Wo Hop, a twenty-four-hour restaurant down a dark flight of stairs in Chinatown. Workers sat at tables, shelling peas or folding wonton skins. After Andrew, in a show of independence, I took a cab there and ate solo, but that was too lonely. Walking away from the restaurant, I turned the corner and came across an older, red-faced man shooting up in a narrow alley behind a garbage can. I never went back.

The East Fifth house specialty was chicken soup that I made for my friends like a good Jewish mama. They all liked it, and it made the tiny apartment a home, cozy and warm. Allen Ginsberg made soup for his friends, too, so I was keeping the Lower East Side tradition. Tradition! The house drink was vodka, since we had such an abundant supply from Daniel's pilfering, preferably mixed with tomato juice. Naturally, dessert was chocolate ice cream.

My parents would come to visit me and my mother would bring homemade fried chicken and chocolate cake. They didn't say it in words, but by the time I was working with Cher, they were somewhat proud of me. My father asked for a photocopy of one of her checks, so he could show his co-workers. At about that time, I started developing an appetite.

A fool! I met a fool in the forest,
A motley fool; a miserable world!
As I do live by food, I met a fool
                      —As You Like It

9

PROFESSORS, TROUBLED IN CALIFORNIA, BACK TO SCHOOL

✑

ONE OF THE FIRST PEOPLE TO BEFRIEND Jill and me in our early New York City days was a photographer and professor of film at the New School. We were strolling along Christopher Street on a beautiful April day and stopped at a card shop. He followed us. "Pardon me, ladies," he said. We were apprehensive and very young, but he seemed nice, in fact, very nice, and he went out of his way not to frighten us. His approach was gentle and businesslike. He was older and a straight-looking straight guy, not at all scary. He introduced himself as Professor Gray and presented his business card. He explained that he worked as a professional photographer and New School professor, and asked if he could photograph us sometime. Over a period of time, he did photograph us together and separately in his plush office and studio in the West Village. This happened gradually. He met our parents and said they were sweet people, but my father didn't like him or the situation. He eyed the professor cautiously without smiling. Gray took hundreds of photos, but never gave us one, and, of course, we were too timid to ask. His Christopher Street space had the feel of the studio in *Blow-Up*, hip and expensive and cozy, but warm. It would have been a cushy place to live, I thought as I washed my hands and burned them on the heated towel rack in the roomy, comfortable bathroom. Jill and I wore button-down oxford shirts, and he took beautiful black-and-white close-ups; I bet he still has those contact sheets stashed away in his files somewhere. He promised to show the shots to someone he knew at *Mademoiselle*.

The professor was married to a beautiful wife and had young children. I met the lovely wife at the well-known class he taught for many, many years at the New School. Gray looked different onstage than he did in real life. His frizzy hair was styled and sprayed into control, and he wore a suit. About six hundred students, mostly professional, affluent people filled an auditorium twice a week. The class viewed the film at a local theater. An actor or director from that film attended the class and discussed it with the professor, followed by questions and comments from the well-heeled student audience. Academy Award-winning director Robert Redford (he won it for *Ordinary People*), and Mark Rydell, director of *On Golden Pond*, spoke of their recent work. It would have been more fun if Rydell had talked about his past role as gangster Marty Augustine, but he wasn't there to do that. Oscar-winning actor Richard Dreyfuss; multi-award winner, composer, songwriter, conductor Marvin Hamlisch; actor Jack Weston;

and Emmy Award-winner James Coco were some other guest speakers. Seeing and listening to these people up close, and being part of the audience was marvelous, something to tell friends.

I had an open invitation to go to the professor's class whenever I liked to see the guest, hear the discussion, and once in a while be invited with a group to a dinner with a famous personality. I brought my friend Randolph Freds, another time David from work came, maybe Andrew came once. Jill never wanted to and didn't like the professor. She was shrewder about people than I. Jill possessed a better sense of people than I did.

Now and then, the professor gave us a little gift: a set of makeup brushes, a lithograph. Once in a while, he bought me something to eat at a coffee shop by his office. He dispensed fatherly advice, called Rand a counter-culture type, and told me I should be dating young doctors and lawyers. I took that as a remark by an older person who didn't understand. Besides, Randolph stood out as a great guy. Rando had been kind from the moment Jill and I met him at CBGB long before. Rand kept an eye on me at Max's; he'd listened when I poured out the unhappy events about Marc and the Creatures and the drinking and the Phil Spector trip to California. Rand, with just a sympathetic raised eyebrow or gentle pat on the shoulder, lifted my spirits; he was not counter. He was *good*, and he was real.

For a while, Gray talked to David about the possibility of his doing work as a guest makeup artist on a cruise line, but that got as far as the deal with *Mademoiselle*. Ambitious, cynical, more of-this-world David grew excited about the prospect, and I was pleased that things seemed to be coming together.

Working six days a week, and working freelance, wore me down. I was exhausted. Randolph and Zeus had a band and a lawyer-manager who had a house in the Hamptons. One weekend, they stayed there and asked me to come along. All I had to do was take the Jitney Express from Manhattan. I looked forward to escaping the East Village seediness for a nice day, or weekend, at the quiet seashore. I envisioned a fireplace and walks on the beach. The long ride out stretched by, relaxed, without any traffic. Good old Rand met me at the drop-off, and we proceeded. The house itself was a modest ranch but without heat; actually, the electricity had been turned off for the winter. A portable heater sat in the center of the room, so that's where we spent our time, under blankets in front of that thing, just kind of talking. Now, Rando was the nicest guy, very pleasant, gentle, and patient. I'd always felt safe with him. He was, however, probably the poorest guy. He was a musician, and I don't remember him ever having any other job; the same was true of Zeus. They had no money, and there was no food in the house except a bottle of whisky. The day went on and got colder and colder, and darker and darker, and then we got hungry. In fact, since I hadn't had anything to eat all day except for a cup of water offered to me on the Jitney Express, I was swooning, downright ravenous, but I was too polite and embarrassed to say anything. Hungry gripped me; I had no energy to even talk anymore. Famished, I took nourishment from the whisky bottle, but hated the taste, so I had just a sip. What seemed like an eternity later, either they called their manager, or the manager called them, and someone came up with the finest idea of the day: a pizza to be delivered and signed for at the house. Oh! How I thanked the heavens for the food soon to be had! The words "pizza delivery!" gratefully rang in my head all the way to my empty stomach. I was never so happy to have food in my life. It was bliss to devour my hot, crusty, luscious slice in that cold, dark house. Randolph and Zeus were both big guys, so I couldn't do what I wanted, which was to eat the whole scrumptious pie, and it was only one pizza. We could have used at least three. After the feast, I hightailed it out of there onto the Jitney and went back to the wintry city without ever seeing the blue, blue ocean.

After the Andrew incident, I felt lonely and decided to go talk to the mature, caring professor at his safe, comfortable office. I had known him for some years and thought he was a friend. He had never done anything for me to think otherwise. I wore a ladylike skirt and my low-heeled alligator shoes. I had grown; I was getting all grown-up by then.

Well, during the conversation, still talking, Gray sank to his knees and started to take his pants down. I froze. Then, he lowered his underpants and began fondling himself while he looked at me. I could not breathe. He reached for my leg.

I slowly rose from my seat and said, "Good-bye, nice to see
you, thanks for your counsel," and hurriedly rushed out,
stunned and so very disappointed. He was like a weird
Woody Allen, and finally, I saw my resemblance to the wide-
eyed Mia. Had he lost his mind? How could he have done
that? Why hadn't I seen it coming? I braced myself against
the cold brick wall of a building and felt sick. I never told
anyone what happened, not even Jill, and never saw Gray
again.

Eventually, the class became a television program, but I
didn't watch it. *People* magazine ran a feature on him. Photos
showed him smiling and surrounded by his family, the beautiful wife and adorable children. He hand-made wooden toys
for them, the article stated. The professor always advised his
class to be polite and stay to read the credits at the end of the
film. Those credited had spent years of their lives to complete
the work. He also urged everyone to be his or her own critic
and not to read the critics before seeing a movie, and I'd listened to him.

A couple of other professors from the past popped up in
my mind. During the time of Mills the dangerous predator,
we worked at a summer job with a research team from the
Department of Wildlife and Forestry at Rutgers. The project
was located in the New Jersey Pine Barrens, a unique natural
area that covers over a million acres in southern Ocean
County. The group took the long drive south in the morning,
and gathered and weighed acorns all day. The researchers

were to determine how the deer population fed. The work stretched out tediously, the day long, hot, and sticky, but the students were devoted to their task. The person heading the project was a hip, groovy, middle-aged man with a lovely middle-aged librarian girlfriend that he cheated on constantly. Naturally, the hip professor also dated his young students.

Elizabeth was a homely graduate student from the Midwest who looked a lot like the woman in Grant Wood's *American Gothic*. She was married to a professor in that same animalistic wildlife department. Her husband was a raging alcoholic. When he drank, he beat her without mercy. She told me all about it, but she still wanted to have a child with him. At the end of my time with the dangerous predator, Elizabeth provided me with comfort and shelter. She lived in a farmhouse with three other grad students, all intelligent and kind, and I, a teenager, stayed there with them one night and thought they were going to have good lives, and I might have a bad one. I wanted to get from where I was—running from the predator Mills—to where they were, safe behind a world of books.

Wolves come clad in professors' robes, too.

My father was a handsome, reserved intellectual with a fine, chiseled face. In his college yearbook photograph, he resembles a young Gregory Peck. He wrote poems to my mother before they were married and remained an original thinker, unafraid to go against the grain; he never quite bought into the whole idea of the materialistic American dream, and definitely not life in the suburbs. His interest lay in the wider world, and he kept abreast of politics, history, and world situations. He was urbane, loved the vitality of cities, lived in a metropolis his entire life, and cared not for backyard cookouts or lawnmowers. He had no interest in maintaining a house, so we lived in an apartment on the waterfront of Perth Amboy. My father invested his money, time, and energy in other ways. To see the world was important to him, and my parents traveled often. My father had a great love of music, preferably live music and dancing, and enjoyed the finer things in life.

As one of the baby boomer generation, my siblings and I were in a distinct minority. We were the last of the children to be brought up to be seen and not heard. We grew up in a city, in an apartment, and my mother didn't drive. We weren't part of the car culture or suburbanites. We watched little television and ate very little junk food. I knew how to survive, thrive, in a city; I had no experience of life outside one, so when my boss sent me from East Fifth Street to a California suburb for two weeks to learn about a new skin-care line, I was lost and culture-shocked in a way the Bowery never made me feel.

My boss was a kind and gracious man who treated me as an amusing, delicate, young innocent. If he knew how events were about to unravel in California, he never would have sent me, or he would have sent Jean, the manager, along. The trip started with me being bounced from a Sunday morning flight at JFK. I waited until the next available plane left that evening at 8:00. In the terminal, only a hot dog stand was opened. I ate a pretzel. By departure time, I was at the breaking point, starving and exhausted by boredom, and frustrated after the long day. Finally, the plane boarded. An unfortunate young man sat next to me. When he tried to start a conversation, I bit his head off. "Please! Shut up! I have a terrible headache." Not a peep came from him for the rest of the flight, and I broke down in tears waiting for the day to end, up, up, and away.

Hours later, I reached the hotel in Huntington or Long Beach or Newport; the classes were in one of those locations. The skin-care line promoted items to separate customers from their money in the hopes of achieving lovely skin. My boss's associate, a middle-aged man with a toupee and convertible sports car, took me to Disney Land one California evening. It was smaller than I had anticipated, there wasn't much to do there except buy merchandise I didn't want. Ironically, I had been there before, either as a tiny infant or *in vivo*. My parents and two older sisters had lived in Orange County briefly, but my mother'd been homesick. After I was born in California, of all places, the family had moved back to Perth Amboy.

A cheery young woman from the class, gung-ho on selling skin-care products, took me out with her friendly friends for an afternoon in the hot California sun, and then we went on a house-hunting expedition another day. I got quite a tour of big houses with big price tags and sleek cars and fiberglass powerboats. I had a feeling it wasn't the Bowery anymore. The consumer excesses and lifestyle on display in California jarred me. Acquisitions were not my priority. I called Jean and told her I was lonely. Don't worry, she assured me. Her boyfriend happened to be in L.A., and she sent the mad, gregarious singer from the Reverend James Cleveland's chorus to show me around one soft crazy-town night. He drove like a maniac. The car hurled forth without touching the road. The radio blasted, and he sang his joyous song and danced a wild man's dance in his seat while grinning at me. I sat, held onto the side of the car with one hand, dug my nails into the plush fabric with the other, and positioned my toes like suction cups on the floor. I reverted to my old timid self. I was far from home and with an out-there stranger in a strange place, no taxis, nothing familiar, with thoughts of the distant, not altogether pleasant Ramones trip in my mind. When we stopped at a convenience store, I asked him to take me back to the hotel, thinking that Jean was nuts.

Other than those unsuccessful outings, I was on my own. I had no car, and even if I drove, I wouldn't have known where to go on the ribbons of freeways. The services at the hotel were limited. The food was mediocre and the service slow, but sunny in the California style. Bored, sad, alone, I watched *The Good, the Bad, and the Ugly* over and over for two weeks. It seemed to be the only program available. I hated Westerns. I experienced some kind of withdrawal, a panic attack. I lost all my mirth and sank into a deep depression.

I had lots of time to think and thought bad thoughts. No one cared about me. I was angry, angry with Andrew the rat. I was annoyed with Jean for sending the madman, and furious at my boss for sending me to California. I didn't care about skin-care products or to be a handmaid for people I found shallow to ridiculous for the rest of my life. Along with the ridiculous, at work I was meeting an emerging breed of professional woman. I needed to get an education and had a lot of catching up to do, being that high school had provided me with so little. I was going to quit my job and stay far away from Andrew. That meant forfeiting New York and moving away from my friends.

In that depressed state, I boarded a bus to a shopping mall and bought all kinds of clothes that I didn't want and would never wear, Western things: suede boots, a denim cowboy shirt, and suede moccasins. I called Jean on the phone, poured out my unhappiness and frustrations, and told of all the money I spent. She cleverly suggested padding my expense account. Jean always had creative ideas. Jean was my dear friend, a mother figure, so surely she meant no harm to her Miss Dumb Bunny. Surely she meant fudging just a little bit, but if you're going to be a jackanapes, you might as well do it with a bang. Being inexperienced in the ways of embezzlement, I did it in such a transparently bogus way that, when I got back to New York, naturally, my boss questioned me. Hangdog, I confessed what I had done; he was very gentle and kind, understood I was lonely, and said, "Don't worry, we'll work it out."

I said, "No. I'm leaving. I'm going back to college."

He looked perplexed; I shook my head and said a sad good-bye. He was a thoughtful person who had given me a big break, and I'd paid him back by being an ingrate.

The move from New York is blocked from my memory. It would have been too emotional to ask my father to help me, and Daniel was with his new friends. I didn't want to impose on Matthew, who'd asked me to share an apartment with him. He was more than I could handle, and I declined his offer. It would have been my last ride in Gian Franco's fabulous automobile, but I didn't have the heart to ask. Randolph and Jean had no cars. My spirit broke. It seems someone I didn't know helped me. Maybe it was a friend of one of my sisters who had a van. My belongings were few, as I tried living by the motto: less is more. Things left behind in the apartment included the mattress and the custom-made wall furniture from Matthew. I discarded the useless Western clothes. (Years later, out of nostalgia, on a trip to East Fifth Street, I noticed that, on the two south-facing windows of the apartment the same bamboo shades I had installed so long before were still hanging.)

I moved back home with my parents. They were kind, and I humble; the prodigal daughter, failed white-collar criminal, and unsuccessful artist, the penitential Magdalene, not quiet Donatello's *Maddalena*, had returned. Jill was on the verge of marrying a businessman, and the little bird flew off. At one time, Paul played drums in a band at CBGB, but he was a smart, realistic sort and had a bright future ahead of him outside the music world. He was a gem.

I enrolled in the county college and decided to forego being an artist. My goal was to do something practical: write and work in publishing. I studied hard to make up for lost time, then transferred to a small women's liberal arts college.

James of the marriage proposal stepped in, but I refused his offer, poor sad-eyed James and his softhearted unrequited love. Another admirer, a rare find: a handsome and educated boy, sterling in all ways, faithful and filled with integrity, proposed at the same time. I refused him as well. I couldn't allow myself to be sidetracked. I needed to complete something. I needed to have that diploma and to tie all the crazy, loopy ends together in some kind of package. That rare talented young man drew a fine likeness of me in charcoal, and he managed to capture my shy smile and spirit. It remains one of the few earthly possessions that I treasure. We had had a successful friendship, and that was important. It represented maturity and growth, but we also needed to part, a sad, realistic finale.

Earning a college degree was paramount. My first goal had always been to live in New York. I wanted experiences and wasn't too concerned about the outcome. I had always managed to pick myself up, after the dust had settled, but I was getting older by then, and more real. Graduating from college was my second goal in life, and I had a steely determination to achieve it. With a how-to book, I learned to type. *Ciao, Manhattan!*

I had gone out into the world and entered into all its noise and clamor in the big city. Uptown, downtown, midtown, I'd met the good, the bad, and the ugly. I had been seduced by glamour and the era of drugs and sex and rock 'n' roll. *Basta.* I longed for peace and quiet and a journey inward. Somehow,

I'd always known I would attend the convent college. I don't know why. I had never even seen a picture of it. I wasn't religious. I knew little about religious sisters or how they lived. When I was very little, I remember nuns strolling in the dusk along the waterfront. White coifs and black veils and stiff black coverings had concealed their faces, their feet shod in black oxfords. They had worn long black habits and rosaries, and I had been mesmerized. My father had told me not to stare. I hadn't understood what they did but found it totally absorbing and mysterious. As little children, we'd attended Christmas and Easter Mass at the Roman church of my mother, and Orthodox Christmas and Easter services at the Russian Orthodox Church of my father. That'd been it. Our parents hadn't sent us to catechism classes. I'd gone to church on Good Friday with my little pale milk-and-vitamin girlfriend and her mother. They lived next door to a sweet German Protestant woman who in the summertime taught a Bible class on her screened-in-porch that overlooked the park and bay. She served us lemonade and cookies and gave us pretty illustrated cards inscribed with scripture verse. My grandmother kept a large painting of St. Thérèse de Lisieux in her bedroom. The Little Flower cradled a cross and roses in her arms. *La Vie en Rose*. And, of course, there was the epiphany of Michelangelo's *Pieta*. That was my religious education.

The small, all-women's college run by a religious order proved a lonesome place, but the campus possessed a fairytale beauty. Old stone mansions, statuary, walls, and gates, and Italian and formal and Japanese gardens with a teahouse, made it enchanting along with the red and golden leaves of fall, the pristine snow blankets and sparkling ice of winter, and the lush blooms of spring. The private girls' school I had hoped to attend in high school was the sister school to the college. In a way, my long-ago high school wish came true. By then, I was older than most of the sheltered baby-girl students and uninterested in the older re-entry women, mostly suburban housewives.

Racee was the one exception to the makeup of the student profile, a wild child who, ironically, had attended a prestigious girls' high school I would have loved. She didn't give two hoots about it. I met her the first day of school. She stood in the circular driveway yelling at her father, "Come on, Dad. Let's go!" She called to me, "I'm Racee!" She laughed and then talked a blue streak and, in a matter of minutes, filled me in on her life story. I made a mental note to keep away from her at all costs.

Racee's father contributed to Covenant House—the agency that provides shelter to runaway youth—because he was sure that would be her destination. She would have cherished that type of drama. However, a more mundane photo shows Racee happily tossing leaves up in the air. She was always moving, fast, rush, rush, rush, on to the next thing. She liked me. She loved the part about the Ramones and my living in the big, bad city, and hoped to involve me in her antics. Occasionally she did, but for the most part, I didn't care to be bothered. By her first semester at the women's college, she was bored silly and wanted out.

In appearance, Racee could have passed for Cher's baby sister. She appeared bone thin, and her hair sprang a wild bird's nest of tight curls, but she drew her long black hair out tight and gathered it in a big bunch on top of her head. She ate sparingly and subsided mostly on black coffee, which she drank by the pot. Her diet, a few bites of a plain bagel for breakfast, tuna for lunch, and broccoli and a little pasta for dinner, all washed down by pots and pots of coffee, kept her marginally sustained and wired day and night.

"I rode around naked with my friend Rich in Morristown. He has a big truck." Racee laughed. I needed to study but picked my head up to look at her. She rolled on the bed, chuckling, "Whoa-ho!" and then "O-O-O! . . . I'm getting tired of Rich. I like this guy I met at Slippery Rock U. I went there on a full ride, full scholarship. I was good in track, but I got kicked out. My GPA was 0. I didn't go to any of my classes. I just hung out in the woods, drinking beer in old mason jars. Whoa-ho! It's the biggest party school. O-O-O! Hey, could I borrow your car this weekend to go to Pennsylvania? I want to see him." She stopped rolling and looked at me dead on.

"No." I put my head back in my book, but being nine years older than Racee, I tried not to hurt the sensitive feelings under the layers of craziness.

Of course, she managed to get to Pennsylvania—or Long Island, where he lived— and came back with a report. She banged on my door. "G! Let me in! Oh, this guy has the

biggest bat, and we smoked pot and had a blast." She collapsed on my bed and laughed. "My roommate stinks. Can
we be roommates?"

That was completely out of the question. "No," I said. "I
need a lot of time to study. I can't have distractions."

"Okay. See you later."

She was slightly defeated but never for long.

Once in a while, I went to her room. Out of sheer boredom, Racee jumped up and down on her bed with a broom-
stick and punctured holes in the dorm ceiling. "G, watch
this!" She didn't stop until she saw the wreckage and sank
into the pillows, laughing. I'm ashamed to admit, her display
was so insanely out-of-control and over-the-top that I burst
out laughing, too, the way I did when Marc went nuts on the
phone with his landlord and Monte. Tears streamed down
my face. What can I say? I always liked the class clowns, the
mad ones. Her roommate's mother raged when she saw the
damage. "*Squirrels* can get in now!" she shrieked. Racee exploded in fits of mirth. I left holding my sides. The school
officials handled the incident calmly, and Racee paid for dam-
ages.

Within a couple of days, she came back. She rambled
about her different adventures. I listened. The campus was
situated on a lake with a perimeter that took us an hour to
walk together. She chattered the whole time; I walked. We
came upon Hasidim in black suits with white shirts and prayer
shawls and black hats, and woman modestly attired in long
dresses with covered heads, and young children in step, babies

and children old enough to push their carriages. "Maybe that's what I should do," Racee mused. "Join a community and have my life mapped out for me without having to make any choices." She looked pensive.

Her parents thrilled that she had latched on to me. I was less than thrilled and tried not to encourage her, but sometimes she got the best of me. Racee's parents were always kind and hoped I would be a good, stable influence on her, but she had a lot of growing to do on her own. She was fearless, more than willing to go the extra mile to meet trouble, and looked forward to whatever scene played around the bend.

At night, Racee cranked up her stereo and played loud funky stuff—Rick James; she stood on the desk in front of large dorm windows that looked out onto the quiet hundred-and-fifty-acre, pine-tree-covered campus and danced—wild crazy gyrations. She threw open the windows and flipped the lights off and on and yelled down to my room, "Hey, G! O-O-O! What the frig's up?" Racee could put on quite the show and could be very funny.

She waxed enthusiastic about all things New York, and we went together to the Village and met my old friend Randolph. In the neighborhood, I took her to see Andrew at his shop as one might take a child to see a monkey at the zoo. I told her all about Andrew and the girls and his leather pants and how he had called my mother to tell about the mafioso and how he had ruined my hair, but I didn't tell her about the broken nose. I was too ashamed to tell even been-there, done-that Racee. She didn't like him, either. "Wow, G. What an ass! You should have had his legs broken." He had changed his Paul McCartney look to hip cowboy dude and had long hair and a white hat.

After the weekend was over, she came back. The familiar rap shook my door, and then she barged in laughing. "Hey, G., mind if I smoke?" Without bothering to hear my reply, she whipped out a joint.

Now that she had my attention, I said, "Open the window. Smoke out the window, so we don't get in trouble." It didn't help. The room ripened with the smell of pot, and the odor lingered all night. The girls at the end of the hall—five or six crammed into a pigsty of clutter with clothes and cereal boxes and old donuts and junk food piled to the ceiling—asked me with glee the next morning, "What was going on in your room?" Those silly girls were all in love with a band called Bon Giovanni, Bon Joy Boy, Bon Bon Boys. (I wasn't in love with any band.) Music cranked full volume, and someone beneath the rubble always seemed to emerge from stale blankets clad in damp sweat clothes. The wafting marijuana wasn't a smart thing, because my room was next to the suite of one of the sisters who just happened to be the college president.

Racee worked fast. She came in. "Hey, G., we should go to Florida, go to the beach, see the palm trees. We could stay with my mom's friend Mrs. Neilly."

Without taking my eyes off the book, I mumbled, "Yeah, Racee, good idea."

"See you later," she said and left in a flash.

Back she came shortly thereafter. "Okay, G., it's all done.

My mom got us the plane tickets." That's how the trip to Florida was arranged.

Mrs. Neilly was a gentile country-club lady married to a single-malt scotch-drinking, cigar-smoking husband. The blonde Mrs. Neilly carried on an affair with her doctor. Undisturbed, Mr. Neilly lounged on the terrace for most of the day and well into evening, drinking and smoking, catching the ashes from his cigar in a coffee can. Once in a while, he rose from his perch and threw bread into a pond where an alligator lived. The Neillys had four beautiful grown daughters. Each lovely blonde was unhappily married to a doctor, but they had been raised to marry that way.

Poor Mrs. Neilly didn't know what she was getting herself into by providing her lovely home to Racee and her friend for a week.

The first day progressed smoothly; we went to the beach and sat near the palm trees. "Just like Gilligan's Island!" Racee said, whooping it up, whoa-ho-ing and O-O-O-ing, but it was cold, and she didn't like the pelicans swooping past. Mrs. Neilly took us to dinner at the "Golden Age of Radio" singer Frances Langford's Polynesian-themed restaurant in Jensen Beach, a corny old-timer place. Racee thought it a hoot, though she probably never heard Frances sing a bang-up "Chattanooga Choo-Choo" in the *The Glenn Miller Story*. However, Racee smiles brightly in the photos, hilariously falling off her chair with the-oh-so-elegant Mrs. Neilly besides her.

By the second day, she waned. "Let's rent a car and drive

to Disney." We took the two-hour drive, walked around the park for forty-five minutes, and that was that. "What a rip-off!" Racee fumed. "We should have gone someplace else." On the grumpy ride back, we pulled off the main highway and found an old-time general store. In the surrounding fields, migrant workers were picking crops. A pre-Civil War scene lay before us, and we were both stunned. "Let's go in and get a drink." On the dusty wooden counter of the store sat a big cloudy glass jar filled with pigs' knuckles. "Man!" Racee mumbled. We had stepped into a strange world. "Let's get out of here, G." We drove back to the Neillys. "How was your day, girls?" Mrs. Neilly asked in her pleasant sing-song voice.

"It was a frigging waste of time!" Alarmingly straightforward Racee never pulled punches.

"Why don't you girls try Mr. Laff's tonight? You might have fun."

We went to Mr. Laff's, a restaurant that had music after a certain hour. Crazily, we danced and did have fun. Someone invited us to a party at a millionaire's beach house, where we met a girl who had gone to Slippery Rock. Racee and the girl hit it off with a bang. "Let's all go to the county fair tomorrow night." Okay. At the fair, the hay smelled fresh, the greased-pig catch progressed, and well-groomed farm animals graced their stalls. Racee met some rubes, two hicks, country bumpkins, who rode hot rods. They looked kind of sly and silly, and I grew apprehensive, not wanting any part of them. "Let's take the boys to Mr. Laff's!" Racee said, all wound up.

"O-O-O!"

I had had enough of Mr. Laff's. "Racee, I'm tired and going to bed," I said.

"Okay, G. You take the car home. I'll go with the boys and my Slippery Rock friend. See you later."

I returned to the Neillys and went to sleep. Later, much later, 4:00 in the morning, Racee stormed into our room and turned on the lights. "G.! I had the worst time! Those frigging boys split and left us at Mr. Laff's, and we had no way to get home. I had to call Mr. Neilly, and he had to drive my Slippery Rock friend home, and then we drove home. And he drove all the way smoking that stink-bomb cigar of his! It was cold, and I had to keep the window open the whole time!"

Poor Mr. Neilly—he hadn't deserved to be awakened by Racee in the middle of the night. "Racee," I said slowly, trying to contain my annoyance, "turn the light off and go to bed." I turned over and put my head under the pillow.

"I froze with that window opened," she continued to herself. "Mr. Neilly and those stupid cigars. Stinking up the whole car."

In the morning, the Neillys were too gracious to mention the preceding night, and thankfully, it was our last day there. For our final dinner, Mrs. Neilly set a beautiful table with her best crystal, linens, and china. Cooking wasn't something Mrs. Neilly did, so we nibbled at the inedible, semi-thawed food and unhappily drank chilled white wine from gorgeous long-stemmed glasses. Racee, in a funk, was still fuming about the boys and the stinking cigars.

When I got home, I sent the Neillys flowers and a letter of apology.

By Racee's second semester, she had been asked to leave the college. Even though she was mostly a nuisance, I did miss her a little. When she wasn't manically depressed, she could be highly entertaining, and we had some funny times laughing and making noise. Racee was a loyal friend and made an attempt to fix me up with her father's co-worker. "G.," she promoted him, "this guy can wine and dine you!" I wasn't interested and didn't like the slick, too-old Jersey guy she had sent my way, but I politely endured a dinner, and then politely said good night. Please don't call me again.

I had had enough relationships and, for the time being, was satisfied studying English literature and visiting the nearby coast. It was not the Jersey shore of summer with its crowds and noise, traffic, heat, sunburn, and manufactured amusements. It was the moody off-season shore with few people, squawking sea birds, brisk salt air, empty beaches, and pounding surf. It was then that I fell in love with the shore: the goldenrod and cumulus clouds of autumn, the snow on the beaches of winter with a brilliant far-away sun, and the cold blue of the vast ocean. Gray days didn't stop me from going, but the visits ended in spring with the conclusion of the school term.

Racee next moved to Boston, where she took a job with a doctor at Harvard that entitled her to take classes there. She quickly blew that opportunity and became involved with a druggie, and then another druggie, had an abortion, and then moved back to New Jersey. I hadn't seen her in a few years when, out of the blue, I received a postcard from her: *G., my brother died last night from a heroin overdose, and I went into early labor and had a baby. Love, Racee.* Good old Racee, never one to waste words, just burn, burn, burn.

School wasn't the same with Racee gone. Eventually, I did make friends with a sweet elderly nun who taught American history, and we stayed in touch for many years by writing and with an occasional phone call or visit. Her goal was to visit all the presidential libraries, and the last I heard, she was going strong. I saved her letters and cards beautifully written in her fine hand. My other school friend was a milky baby girl who still held hands with her mother while crossing the street.

One professor at the school awed me. Maria Bella Cuore was a unique person: highly educated and refined, beautiful, and mysterious. From halfway across the room, she appeared to be in her thirties. Suora Bella was in her sixties and one of the few sisters who still wore the habit. The modified habit— simple black dress and veil—looked elegant and worthy of respect as well. She was a poetess and Chaucerian scholar, a gentle, demure lady, and probably the most beautiful, unadorned woman I have ever seen. Her poised presence commanded like that of a very great stage actress; she was brilliant and fluent in French and knew Latin. She knew the great poets and the Psalms and literature of the Bible, and could flawlessly recite quotations from both by memory. "Don't consider yourself an educated person," she cautioned, "unless you know the Bible." It was quite an experience to have so charming a woman, a veiled nun, teach the *Canterbury Tales*. Above the wood-paneled library wall in the main mansion on campus hangs a fine mural of the Canterbury pilgrimage, painted by Robert Van Vorst Sewell: how perfect a setting for the frieze and for Madame Professor. With a firm turn of her key, she opened the door to the giants: Chaucer, Shakespeare, and Milton, followed by distinguished literary others through the centuries. With nothing from high school but what I had scraped together on my own from piecemeal self-learning at the library and life experience, I entered into a sanctuary of higher education.

Maria of the Beautiful Heart's mystery was, we knew little about her. Her yearbook graduation photograph from when she was a student at the college shows her as a cameo beauty, and she bears a resemblance to British actress Vivien Leigh. The girls said she walked with her feet not touching ground. We found a photo, from her doctoral days at Fordham, in which she wears the traditional floor-length habit and full head covering and veils.

Suora Maria Bella held the chair of the department, and in a way I knew her well but never actually got to know her. I saved her many letters and cards. She kept her distance but did write in her exquisite, ladylike, fourteenth-century hand in blue ink, in the pristine white margin of one of my papers, that I had "true writing talent." Fellow students said Suora Maria and I were alike. After my turbulent past, I wasn't so sure, but it was a heartfelt compliment and reassuring to hear they thought well of me. I didn't talk about the past much, because I wanted to forget it. The past is perfect because it cannot be changed, and mine was perfectly imperfect, marred to a rich patina that comes with years.

One of the last of his breed, an old-school professor, an elderly, cantankerous master who had retired years before from Rutgers, taught at the college. His physical appearance was not too different from Louis Auchincloss's *The Rector of Justin*, not much difference at all: "short. . . , noble square head. . . , thick shock of stiff, wavy grey hair. . . ." Our literary lion had authored a book on the Bard, published in 1938, and we were required to troop over to the little campus library to have a look at the one copy the library kept under careful cover.

We read and memorized passages from *Antony and Cleopatra*, *Coriolanus*, *Hamlet*, *Macbeth*, *Othello*, and *Romeo and Juliet*. One by one, we stood in his small office and gave it a shot. Professor Snarky MacGruff hunched in his swivel chair at his desk with hands clasped and white head bent down, concentrating. No sound came forth until he gave a grunt, and that was that. Getting to know Shakespeare took work. The language is centuries old. "Listen to the language! These are plays. The words are meant to be heard!" he scolded.

The college's small library had one record of Richard Burton reading *Coriolanus*, one of the more obscure plays. That was it, no others. I listened to it and managed to see the in-

frequently produced play at the renowned New Jersey Shakespeare Festival, dedicated to the playwright's canon. Now,
thanks to the marvels of the Internet, reams of user-friendly
information on Shakespeare are available at one's fingertips;
not so then. I struggled but persevered and kept memorizing,
and that pleased the crotchety professor. He didn't say so, but
it warmed his old heart to know that someone cared about
William Shakespeare. During the summer, I wrote to the ancient professor to tell him I had *seen* the play and *heard* the
words of *Coriolanus*. He sent an erudite reply that I didn't
quite understand the first couple of times I read it, but have
preserved as carefully as his old book. In it, he instructs me
to remember that the turning point occurs at the speech, "You
common cry of curs," and I should reread certain passages.

The professor lived at the shore and, regardless of the
weather, heartily swam in the ocean every day, but he was ir-
ritable and once threw a fit in class: "What has *happened* to
you young girls? Why are you not *feminine* any longer? Why
does no one wear *ribbons* in her hair?" Old as he was, he
scared some of us to death. The intrepid Racee feared not—
she could, in her words, "give two flying figs" about Dr. Mac-
Gruff or his class. She didn't have him for a teacher, and if
she had, she would have skipped it. "MacGruff's barking
again!" she laughed as she flopped down on the bed.

As for me, I studied away, and read, and re-read, and then
read again. I studied as if my life depended on it. I studied to
make up for all my past transgressions, and it paid off: I graduated with honors and the highest grades in the English de-

partment.

When MacGruff was on a tear, he started in on poor old Ronald Reagan. "That cowboy in the White House!" he mumbled and grumbled, and most of the girls remained impassive. It was then that he mirrored the theatrics of that great Catholic and lover of Shakespeare, the matinee idol and long-time Count of Monte Cristo, James Tyrone.

MacGruff might end the class by going into raptures about the refined stage tragedienne Katharine Cornell, famous for her 1934 role as Juliet. I'm sorry I didn't get the chance to see her. He thought about those glory days, gradually refocused his eyes on the not-as-impressive young women, sans hair ribbons, who sat silently in front of him, and waved his hand to dismiss his students.

Looking at a few photographs of Suora Bella, twenty years after I graduated from college, I see she wears the habit and remains beautiful. Her white hair peeks out from her black veil. Her posture is erect, and she still has a lovely natural smile that reflects her serenity. She lives behind the walls of the convent, tends the beds of roses and the campus gardens of the one-time estate, reads literature, and writes poetry, eloquent verse in iambic pentameter that will probably never be published or seen by many. She is a devout nun and prays for all of humanity and the long stream of young women who have passed through the convent's narrow gates. A photo shows her in the simple black dress and veil wearing gardening gloves as she kneels down to work the earth.

Age cannot wither her, nor custom stale
Her infinite variety: other women cloy
The appetites they feed, but she makes hungry
Where most she satisfies.

—*Antony and Cleopatra*

Acknowledgments

Special thanks to Thérèse of Lisieux and her shower of roses.

Thanks to Robert James Stritch who planted the seed.

Thanks to Jill who created a bloom of youthful genius.

Thanks to Kris who often went out on a limb for me.

Thanks to Jackie who was firmly rooted and didn't stray.

Thanks to Keven for carrying the weight of the tree.

Thanks to my parents, the rock.

I beg forgiveness, as I have forgiven.

Thank you, Barry Sheinkopf—well done, editor and book designer. Bravo.

Thank you, Kelly Merklin and Andy Puleo for reading.

Accolades to the Wayne Public Library, New Jersey.

About the Author

To know me is to know books,
Far more interesting than my looks.
Decades and decades read and read,
American and Brit Lit runs through me head.
Bios and memoirs, classics too,
Then I wrote one that was true.
And another and another,
Earn my daily bread 'n' butter,
Rejection seventy times seven.
Someday when I get to heaven. . . .
Peaceful bliss sans publishing division,
There I'll bask in the beatific vision.

Photo Gallery

Painting by a thirteen-year-old Cooper Union hopeful (1970)

Hip Swiss boy (1978)

Interior CBGB (1978)

Blonde me (1982)

Jill and our Barbies (1980)

Jill and Bowery boys (1980)

The author and Joey Ramone (1978)

Waiting for the bus to New York City (1978)

Cher sans makeup (1982)

Texas George (1986)

Mezzogiorno piano boy (1982)

East Fifth Street (1981)

Downtown Ciao! Manhattan (1987)

The Mighty Cooper Union (1982)

Aye, Laddie (1994)

Fairy-tale beautiful convent campus (1985)